Speaking in the Language of Angels

By Julia Vazey

Bright Pen

Visit us online at www.authorsonline.co.uk

A Bright Pen Book

Copyright © Authors OnLine Ltd 2007

Text Copyright © Julia Vazey 2007

Cover design by Julia Vazey and James Fitt ©

All rights reserved. No part of this publication may be reproduced, stored in a retrieval system, or transmitted in any form or by any means, electronic, mechanical, photocopy, recording or otherwise, without prior written permission of the copyright owner. Nor can it be circulated in any form of binding or cover other than that in which it is published and without similar condition including this condition being imposed on a subsequent purchaser.

ISBN 0 7552 1063 8
ISBN 978-0-755210-63-3

Authors OnLine Ltd
19 The Cinques
Gamlingay, Sandy
Bedfordshire SG19 3NU
England

This book is also available in e-book format, details of which are available at www.authorsonline.co.uk

Other titles by the same author

Spiritual Essential Series

1. A Holistic guide to Personal growth
2. Past Lives – Your unique journey

Other Titles

On Life, Wisdom and Spirituality Vol. 1.
More On Life Wisdom and Spirituality Vol.2.

Julia Vazey is an Internationally known
Spiritual Educator,
Presenter of Classes and Workshops,
Spiritual Counsellor, Author,
and Newspaper columnist.

Dedication

To my daughter Natasha, who always allowed me, her "Mum", to be the Internationally travelled spiritual educator, facilitator, columnist, author and counsellor that I was guided to be. Even though, this meant we did not see each other for long periods of time.

This book is for her, and her beloved children, Jaden, Kai and Maaia.
My darlings, Nana hopes that in some small measure her life path has made this fantastic world a more peaceful, tolerant and loving place for you to be in.

Acknowledgments

The most important people to thank are those who remained unnamed, yet are the core of the examples and stories in this book. These special people have attended my workshops, had private consultations with me, attended weekly classes and shared their stories, openly, willingly and honestly.

A very special mention for their help, encouragement, and editing skills must go to Alison Strandberg, Sheila Armstrong, Jan Canton.

Contents

Your Spiritual Plan	1
It's not an Occupation	12
You leave when You Choose	18
Angels and Master Souls	24
Your Personal team of Angels and helpers	43
How you can use Your Angels more	57
The Language of Angels	63
Prophecy	70
Clairvoyance	79
Clairaudience	87
Clairsentience	96
Connection and Protection	105
Asking Questions	119
Why we "Appear" to get Wrong Answers	131
Asking Cupid for a Partner	138
Letting Go and Letting god	149
Your Changing Team	165
You are a Light Being	169
You are Creating Heaven on Earth	172

Your Spiritual Plan

You are a soul; A unique vibration of energy. You are an evolving vibrating form of energy that is a part of the whole that fills our galaxy and the galaxies beyond that. You will form, expand, and break away and reform in your quest to experience the magnificence of what you really are. You are an all loving, knowing, understanding piece of what is commonly called God.

However, it is very hard to experience the reality of these ideas while we are living in a world that is full of third and fourth dimensional thinking and limitations. That is, a world that is governed by the three dimensions of space, height, breadth and depth, and the fourth one of time. In universe there are no such constrictions

So why would you leave the joy, bliss, love, peace, and all knowing wisdom to come to such a little place as Planet Earth? It is really quite simple. While you are living in the emotional utopia of the fifth dimension and beyond, it is hard for you to sense, feel, experience and appreciate how glorious you really are.

It is somewhat like you being in a classroom where the students never sat any exams or tests. It makes it very difficult to see what your talents, skills, and capacity is. To be able to really appreciate how wonderful you are you need to be in an environment that offers you lots of contrast.

Planet Earth is one of the few places that you can visit repeatedly and continue to evolve. It is an advanced system of spiritual growth because of the varying levels of consciousness in the people we meet daily. These encounters allow us a measure of how close we are to becoming "One with all Things". When we can live in the state of consciousness of "ONENESS" then, and only then, can we live side by side in harmony with our spiritual brothers and sisters, regardless, of race, creed, religion, education, and financial circumstances.

Yes! But why am I here?
Simply put, you here at this time and space to expand and evolve. You are here because you chose to be here, for not one soul on this Planet is here by accident. Why? because you are in a spiritual system that is motivated by desire. You are here to discover more about yourself through your earthly experiences.

Your life purpose or plan is to experience balance and harmony in specific areas within the all-embracing Universal laws. This makes up the rudiments or basics of your particular path. For example, if you wanted to unfold your capacity for compassion, then you would set up situations that would allow you to have many experiences where compassion, or the lack of it was the core issue. In order for you to feel an immense amount of love you must know what the lack of love feels like.

It takes one end of the scale to reflect the opposite end. For example, night and day, dark and light, up and down. The movie "Unbreakable", starring Bruce Willis taught me a great deal about this concept of antithesis.

We are all here to live within the constant unchanging universal laws that govern the oneness. For example, envisage that any one of the Universal Laws looks like the diagram below.

```
10 ------------------ 0 ---------------10
```
Positive   Negative

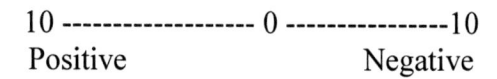

At any given time in your life you will be living this law at some point along the graph. The ultimate idea is that we can maintain and live this law fully at point 10 Positive. This may take many lifetimes to achieve. Some of the laws you will catch onto very easily, yet others will be a real challenge in the face of life in our society here on Earth.

You may have already recognised that some of your friends have a real challenge with the law of Loyalty to Oneself, or the Law of Trust or the Law of Flow (going with the flow). This system of positive or negative growth applies to all the experiences here on the earth plane.

Before you enter earth's realms you have a set of decisions to make. These decisions all relate back to why you have a desire to incarnate at this time. This need to grow, expand, and achieve inner balance and harmony is the underlying factor to all things. So here are some of the key areas you clarified before re-incarnating for this lifetime.

You Create your Physical body
Having decided to come back to earth, you will need to create yourself a physical form. Your body is rather like a rental car – you choose the make, year, size, colour, model, and the country it would be made in. You will "drive" your rental car all around Planet Earth, using it to have your adventures in, and then when you are ready, you will dump it somewhere and go home.

For most of us, we will be forced to leave our "rental cars", because they are worn out, rusty, the headlights don't work so well, the upholstery is all saggy and there are no replacement motors available. At exactly the right time, when we feel ready, we will vacate our physical bodies and go home.

You chose your parents
The next step in your plan was that you entered into a contract with two other souls to make you a physical body and raise you until you were able to take care of yourself. These of course are your parents. You choose your particular parent/parents for the spiritual attachment that you have created with them in the past.

You are there to help your parent/parents to expand their thinking and understanding by your experiences, and of course, they will help you by their views and values. It is seen as a two-way contract. It has to be, as children are not children, but rather wise old souls learning to master a new physical body and the rules of life. Many parents have been forced to change their attitudes and views about life, by the behaviour and life choices of one of their children.

Look at the number of parents forced into being more compassionate, forgiving and understanding by their child having a baby outside of marriage, drug involvement, or illegal activities and brushes with the law. Parents, who have focused their self-acceptance and self worth by their social or financial standing in the community, will often have teenagers that humble them from that lofty exalted pedestal.

Families are meant to be all about loving and encouraging each individual soul into being the greatest person that they can be, regardless of occupation, financial success, or social position. From a spiritual perspective the family unit is meant to be a haven into which we return when our travels on earth wear us down. We come "home" to be safe and to be accepted and loved just because we are who we are.

In some families it becomes very apparent that one parent has a stronger connection or affinity with a particular child. Of course this does not mean that the parent does not love all their other children. It simply shows that these two beings have forged a strong connection in a past life.

I (Julia) was pushing my bike up a hill on a dark night on the way home from being on our regular Friday night outing to the cinema. At the time I was fourteen years old, and not at all athletic like my brother, so he had left me far behind. I was puffing and panting, and only half way up the hill, when there, between the handlebars of my bicycle, appeared the vision of a beautiful face. It seemed to me that the world vanished and nothing existed but this divine face and I. She said to me" I do not care who you marry, but you must call me Natasha".
Her lovely dark hair, big brown eyes, a shadowy mark on her forehead, and the tone in her voice, and her inner glow captivated me. It seemed like I had just adjusted my eyes to looking at her, when she vanished and my surroundings re appeared.
The following year I was struck down with some very mysterious illness, and during my morphine drugged state I became aware that I would never be able to bear children. I just knew that if I were ever to have the joy of raising a child, I would have to adopt one. I was twenty-seven when we adopted our daughter Natasha, and today she looks the same as the vision I had all those years ago, complete with a birthmark on her forehead.

Because I adopted my daughter Natasha, I have been the recipient of the following statements or beliefs by a number of well meaning but very insensitive people.
Statements such as,
The mother obviously was not a good person.
It's a shame you had to take on a child no-one else wanted.
How sad you don't actually have a child of your own.
What a good person you are to take on someone else's child.
Are you sure you haven't bought a barrel of trouble.
Of course, you don't know what she will turn out like with her background.

Need I go on? These remarks were very hurtful and shocking at the time, until I realised how ignorant and lacking in compassion the speakers were. So let's take a look at the situation of adoption from a spiritual and big picture point of view. In fact lets look at two possibilities or scenarios.

1. *There I was, the person she chose to be her Mother, due to an illness at the age of fifteen, rendered unable to make her a physical body. Her plan A. had been blown. So now she has to put into effect plan B. Quickly, she makes a new agreement with another soul to be a Mum and make her a physical body. This soul agrees because they are willing to learn all about the universal law of "letting go". This means she will experience all about loving someone enough to let her go for her highest good. Natasha is duly born to her birth mother, and ends up with me as her Mum, as she always intended.*
2. *Consider yet another scenario altogether. What if Natasha, and I had decided that we both wanted to learn about unconditional love, then this seems a perfect situation to experience it in. I had to come to terms with the emotional growth, which I have to say took many years, of not being able to have a baby of my own. Natasha on the other hand, needed to learn that motherhood is a role, not a position of birth.*

Either way, we belong together as Mother and Daughter this lifetime. I feel we are a dream team. The very fact that she is not of my blood makes me treasure our relationship even more. I am, and always will be, eternally grateful that one very generous and courageous young woman allowed me to experience motherhood with a child she brought into the world.

If you have a great deal of difficulty accepting that you chose your particular set of parents, then it would be helpful for you to look at what they helped you learn about life, families and love. Some childhoods are undoubtedly less than could be desired. Yet, each of these situations will have served to give the child, a valuable perspective on choices about how they might prefer to manage relationships later in life.

In our very westernised and materially focused world, it is easy to get caught in the feeling that your parents did not provide you with the love, life style and support that you wanted. Well the truth is, that if, and you did, chose your parent/parents, you are receiving exactly the love and support that you asked them to give you. This is your plan and path and anything more is a fairy tale.

If you were raised in a single parent family then that is what you chose, so longing for the perfect two-parent family is a huge waste of time. I meet many adult women who are still seeking the love and or approval they believe they did not get from their Fathers. This search has often led them into adult relationships with men who are; Father figures, much older than them, look like their father, or behave the way their father did. This is such a waste of time and energy, and sadly, to add to the emotional pain, most of these unions do not last.

So many people find it easier to blame others like their parents for the way they are, or the situations they find themselves in. This is simply an excuse not to be personally responsible and do what is required to claim and create the life they truly desire and deserve. With all the access to books, counselling methods, workshops, groups and classes, and the Internet, there is no need for anyone to stay ignorant of a larger truth or picture about life anymore.

You chose when and where you were born
The next decision to be discussed with your angels while you are still in the heavenly realms is where and when you will choose to be born. Specifically, it is what country, year, month, and time that you will enter the earth plane. Every

country and culture offers such a diverse range of experiences, that you will have chosen very wisely indeed, keeping your life purpose in mind.

Some of you will have chosen, at a very early age, to go with your parents and leave the country you were born in. However, by your birthright alone, you will have created options that you can use at a later time. For example, if you were born in England, and then returned with your parents to their homeland, you, by right of birth, will have legal access to live in England.

Many souls organize themselves in this way, so that at a later date they will have easier global mobility to do what they have come to do. Furthermore, if your favourite season of the year is the season you were born in, then your parents got your timing just right. Alternatively, if your favoured season is one other than the one you were born into, your parents withheld your birth time, for reasons more convenient or practical to them.

You also chose your experiences
Choosing what you want to experience through people and situations must be the most exciting part of your plan for this lifetime. Every difficult person and circumstance that ever happened to you were in response to a specific request that you made to your angels and God.

Yes, everyone and everything was and is there, at your request, for there is no such thing as coincidences.
The person whom you find the hardest to interact with is the one you have asked to teach you something.
More truthfully they are there to help you discover and experience the "higher Way".
So often I hear stories similar to the following one.

A woman had been dating a gentleman for some months. As time went on she felt that they were not compatible, and were never going to make good partners for each other, so she decided to end the relationship. Each time she told the man that she did not want to see him again he was able to talk or bully her into submission and they would continue to see each other. He would tell her and other people that she was mental, or menopausal, and at the same time he still desperately clung to her. He would beg to come into her home just for coffee and a talk, and she, feeling sorry for him, would agree and the whole process would start all over again. For months she has been trying to get him to accept that it was over between them, to no avail, as he simply will not listen to what she is saying. By now she was so desperate to have closure on the whole affair that she was thinking of moving cities. She believed the problem lay with the gentleman, and so she was shocked when I said it was her problem and challenge to solve and overcome. I suggested that she did not really want him to leave otherwise her resolve to implement and stand by her decision would be immovable. Finally she confessed she did not want to hurt him for it made her feel so guilty. Upon discussion it was clear that she had to decide whom she was living her life for, herself and her own happiness, or someone else's view of life and happiness. He had indeed been a very great teacher for her, just as she had requested him to be.

The only reason that people and circumstances appear in your life is to assist you to have experiences and gain wisdom from the encounter. There are no such things as victims in life, for all things are an act of choice and a step towards empowerment and oneness. Look for the hidden spiritual gems, treasures, and gold in each of your circumstances and you will be amazed at how those "difficult folk" have been master souls and teachers in disguise. Learn to bless the difficult folk for they bring us the richest of treasures, a knowledge of ourselves.

As you add to your own spiritual knowledge, awareness, wisdom and growth, your aura and inner light glows a brighter; your connection with the fifth dimension and the Angelic realms becomes stronger. As each little piece of information ignites a light of recognition in your consciousness.

As a consequence, your flame grows even bigger, and so does your power to be a light worker and change agent here on the physical realm. Never be disheartened that you, as an individual cannot make a difference, for it is not true. It is a vast collection of individually enlightened souls, just like you, that are creating the changes on planet earth.

As the energy on Planet Earth gets lighter and higher spiritually, people are able to unfold their own spiritual awareness through books, audiocassette tapes, cd's, talks, lectures, workshops and even the Internet. In this age you are fortunate to have a smorgasbord of materials and tools to help you grow.

This is the time of the spiritual individual, and people seeking their own way to the universal consciousness. It is a great time of questioning and finding your own truths within, for that is the only place that your particular truth can be found. Trusting yourself and what your sensitivity is telling you, is now, and will continue to be, more important that ever. What is truth for you at your level of consciousness is your truth, and it may not be what others around you can accept or agree with.

At this time the universe is asking you to hold firm, be resolute in your values and beliefs and be an example of light to others who are also seeking to expand their awareness. From time to time be prepared to re-evaluate your beliefs and views by considering a bigger or different picture about people, spirit and life. By being open in this manner your angels and the spiritual masters will be able to channel even greater truths to you about the universe and the path to ascension.

An Angel appears to be like everybody else – only more so

It is not an Occupation

So here and now, lets end one widely held misconception. Your life purpose is "**Not an occupation**". You did no re-enter planet earth to be a plumber, builder, fashion designer, sales person, accountant, lawyer, factory hand, nurse or any other profession or occupation. These are your professions, the ways in which you will discover then utilize, your natural skills to earn an income.

Sometimes you will fall into an occupation that will be very natural and easy for you, yet it may not be the vocation or profession that you have come to utilize this lifetime. I had a client who had a natural gift for horse training, a skill that became apparent at a very early age, to all that knew him. For all his talent at horse training, he was bored, and recognized that this was not his path, and was seeking insights into a new direction.

Your life purpose is actually a spiritual message, an inspirational view or value, a way to live life that will inspire others to do the same. Throughout your life, the universe will present you with opportunities to mix and connect with people. This may be through; Work, Clubs, Sporting activities, Cultural groups and Social situations, all of which will allow you to express your personal spiritual message, your inner views, perceptions, truths and values. This is what you really came to earth to do.

Your personal message is the thing that you came to share with others and it will remind them of one of the many wonderful facets within themselves. It could be one of the many facets in any of the following subjects;

Healing   self-esteem and confidence   compassion
creativity   motivation   inspiration
detachment   manifesting   courage
endurance   self leadership   freedom
or clearing emotional blockages.

Whatever the quality is, it will be the common theme that people feel when they are in your company, as this is the deeper reason that they are spending time with you. Whatever your personal message is, it will be as easy as breathing oxygen for you, and often very difficult for other people to implement in their lives.

They will hold you in awe, reverence and respect, or see you as special or lucky because you have this natural quality or value. You will be an inspiration to others by showing them how this facet of their lives could be managed. This is what I call self or spiritual leadership.

I used to get into trouble in school for always talking when I was not supposed to. Little did those teachers in the 50's know that I was practicing for my life's purpose? I came to speak in front of many thousands of people and I began practising this craft as early as my school years. At this point I would like to apologise to any of my teachers because I was definitely a disruption in many of their well-planned classes. It is interesting to note that my eldest grandson, Jaden, is doing exactly the same thing, and getting into the same kind of trouble I used to.

As you proceed past the age of twenty-eight, you will feel a strong spiritual urge to find an occupation that allows you to share your message with people. Any occupation that you thoroughly enjoy and would be willing to do, whether you were paid or not, is a heavenly blessing. It means that you have found a job, which allows you the freedom to channel your unique message, value or view on life.

Throughout my school years I excelled at essays, stories, poetry. It is a skill I have used over the years to write letters, short stories, and magazine articles.So why should I have been so surprised when my angels suggested I could reach more people by writing books.

I am very creative in my approach about how things can or could be achieved, and for this trait, friends say that I am very positive. I stimulate the creativity within other people, especially if they have an artistic flair. Creativity is simply looking at a situation and finding more than one way to achieve the best outcome or solution. It's a "How can I do this" approach to life. I recognise that I stimulate people to act on their dreams, goals or wishes.

My personal **Life Purpose** it to help people trust their own,
Feelings, sensitivity and instincts,
Reasoning and decision making,
and above all, the messages from their angels/guides and the universal masters.

I realise that the reason for every encounter I have with another human being, is to instil and strengthen this message within them in some way. If you do not tamper with what your Angels/God suggest you do, you will find yourself in the main stream of your own life, spiritually, mentally, physically and emotionally. If they bother to "Suggest" you to do something 3 times, Listen! For goodness sake listen.

Next evaluate the steps needed and then act. Your Angels will not play games with you. If they feel something is for your highest good they will repeatedly indicate it. So! The opposite of tampering, arguing, doubting, and procrastinating on spirits messages is to surrender, act and TRUST. TRUST, TRUST.

When you have "found your life's niche" you will always find a challenge in your work. Whether that challenge is in acquiring new knowledge, by the way of professional development and education, upgrading and expanding your training, or the way in which you present your business to people. For the most part, each day will be like an adventure filled with experiences, understanding, creativity and fulfilment.

It is not always easy to clarify your purpose, just as writing a mission statement for business can be very challenging. You might say that a mission statement is the spiritual purpose of a business or organization. So lets look at some of the possibilities that might shed a little light on your particular life and spiritual purpose. That, hard to define spark that you have, that everyone else feels and is touched by when ever they are in your company.

Ask yourself some of the following questions.
- What is the common thread of your stimulating conversations with other people?
- What do people say they feel when they are in your company
- If you only had one sentence that you could ever say to help people, what would that sentence be?
- What is the common factor in the jobs that you have enjoyed the most?
- What are the most common suggestions that you give people when they share their problems with you?
- What is the quality or habit that people always admire in you?

You could even ask seven friends or family members to answer some of the above questions for you and then analyse the answers. You will have to alter the wording of the questions so they are assessing you and not themselves. There is an old adage that states, "Seven people can't be wrong".

Whether it is true or not, 7 sets of answers should reveal some common things that will give you a basis to start with.

The answers to these questions may begin the process of clarifying your particular spiritual purpose.

Some of the things in my life that gave me clues to my life purpose were that I would always get excited about people who dared to live their dreams. I was, and still am; suffused with energy and enthusiasm when people have the courage to follow their personal inspiration from spirit, and be leaders in their own lives.

My own income-earning path has been an evolving process. It is not a journey that has ever stayed static for very long. My work history would probably be a recruiting agencies worst nightmare.

For example, here are some of the things I have done to earn an income over the years;

Cosmetic sales	Manicurist	Hairdresser
Domestic cleaner	Industrial cleaner	Dressmaker
Shop assistant	Direct marketing	Salesperson

Machinist in an underwear factory
Machinist in a shoe factory
Teacher of special needs teenagers
Assist manager in Pharmacy
Sales team leader of 43 staff in a mobile Florist Business
Teacher in a Hospitality College
Taught arts and craft classes
Facilitated Personal growth programs for the Australian Government.
Facilitated Self Esteem & Confidence classes for State and Private Schools
Owned and operated a garment manufacturing business
Had a partnership in a Motor garage service station
Ran my own International Spiritual Growth business
Presented personal growth programs in prisons
Written and recorded Audio Cassette tapes
Written and produced 5 books on Spiritual growth

Further more, and at the tender age of 61 I am embarking on a whole new job path. The moral of the story is that some of us have come to be very adaptable, flexible and multi-taskers. This is the way the Universe gets us to connect with such a wide and varied range of people. What a bitter disappointment I would feel my life has been if I believed that I "should" ever have only had one job or career.

Instead I treasure the rich tapestry I have woven of my life. I have so loved the variety of opportunities and the rich assortment of people I have met and worked with. Each person and opportunity has given me a chance to discover my skills, talents, and even limitations. The common theme through all my income-earning years has been people. Inspiring them with self-knowledge and self- understanding has been my "food for the Soul". So! Trust your own path, do not compare your journey with that of another's, and above all choose the life you want.

When you are suffused with chills or goose bumps you are surrounded by Angels

You leave when you choose

An integral part of your plan is the time when you will depart the earth plane. If your purpose has been achieved at the age of two months, eight years, twenty years, or eighty- two years, then you will find a way to release your mortal shell and return home. The spiritual value of our time on earth has nothing to do with the years we spend here. A soul who stays 6 weeks then leaves, is as equal in value to a person who stays until they are 100.

Nobody departs from the earth realms unless they decided to do so. From the moment we are born, we are all on the journey towards our death or transition; all that is questionable is "when" this will take place.

Having been to planet earth many times before, you really do "know" that, at times, it gets really difficult to remember that we are just passing through this plane. We are often weighted down by the sheer weight of the rights and wrongs, do and don'ts, and the should and should nots that exist here on Earth. Sometimes, the expectations of family, partners, friends and society can be so overwhelming, that it's just so hard to see the light at the end of the tunnel. I call these times the dark nights of the soul.

For this reason, you build in escape routes into your plan, times when you can leave the planet if you choose too. These are times when illness, an accident, or any other tragedy allows you the option to pass on if you want too. For you, it might have even been a very close call in a potential car accident. You may even be a survivor in a motor accident, boating incident or fire. On any one of these occasions you may have opted to return home to the universe.

It is spiritually normal to feel so much despair about the events or circumstances in your life that leaving the earth plane seems utterly preferable. At these times it seems as if all the light in the world has gone out, and all hope is lost. All it means is that you can no longer see the reason or purpose for the events surrounding you, and your own direction. The key is to find someone, a book, a meditation or prayer that will reconnect you again to that light within.

I was just a toddling three year old when My Mum and I were travelling by bus to Nelson to visit my uncle. I have no recollection of being ill, but it seems I took a turn for the worst on the bus, resulting in the driver taking all the passengers on a detour to the hospital, so that I could be admitted for treatment. I was highly feverish and constantly crying.

That night I clearly remember deciding that I wanted to leave planet earth and return to God. I got out of bed, walked along the ward, letting myself out through the double doors. I proceeded across the frosty grass in my bare feet, determined to walk until I reached God. A nurse caught up with me and asked, "Where are you going? My curt reply was, "I am walking to God, because I don't want to stay here any more. It doesn't feel very good".

The nurse then reminded me of my life purpose by saying, "You can't go now, there is a little girl in the bed next to you who needs you to help her. She can't feed herself and you could do that for her". So, reluctantly, I agreed to walk back into the hospital ward with her, and from that day until I was discharged I fed the child in the bed next to me.

Years later I was to find out that my parents had lost a child (my sister Helen) to meningitis at this time, and I believe I was feeling the overwhelming pain of their grief. To me, returning to God seemed a preferable option. All these years later, I am still not sure if a real nurse found me or if it was one of my angels masquerading as a nurse that came to my rescue. Since then there have been several times when I recognize I could have exercised my option to leave, but instead I have chosen to stay on. These major crossroads or hurdles have been the catalyst for great changes in my life.

Because we are not privy to each other's spiritual plans it can be very difficult to understand the reason for some people's lives, and their way and time of departure. So much pain can be avoided, and understanding gained, if we just looked at people as evolving souls on a spiritual journey or quest. This quest will inevitably lead us to leave the earth Plane

In one particular year, here in New Zealand, we had three separate incidents where children aged between nineteen months and four and half years old, died from extreme physical cruelty and abuse. The stories that emerged through the media about the plight of these small defenceless toddlers, was both horrifying and gut wrenching. The whole nation was rocked by these three events, which occurred within a six-month time frame. Suffice to say that the uproar these deaths caused, was enough to change the way our, doctors, police, hospitals, and social welfare departments handle any glimmer of child abuse now. Among the people in my classes and workshops the most frequently asked question about these events was, "How could God let this Happen?" and the answer is, God did not. These three "little children" were not little children, but rather immense spiritual beings, who together, agreed to come into their particular family environments and circumstances. Their collective purpose was to show a nation what has been happening, undetected, and behind closed doors, for a very long time. Had they not come in as a gateway of energy, agreeing to pass on within close proximity of each other, there lives and deaths would have been in vain. Instead their lives served to illuminate an area in our nation that needed major legal, social and community reform.

Many families get lost in the tragedy and grief of losing a child, in what seems to be the flower of its youth. To the parents, there is no logic, rhyme nor reason for this child, with its whole life ahead of it, to die so young. If the parents could see the spiritual bigger picture of their precious infant, they would realise that it was not a child, but a huge wise old soul. It has chosen to leave the earth realm and continue it's glorious quest. Perhaps then, honouring their small part in each other's journey would be cause, not for prolonged grief, but rather for a celebration of life, love and sharing.

I have even seen the glorious dark shimmering Angel of death, whom I prefer to call the Angel of transition, who has chosen to help us make the transition from the physical world to the Spiritual one. This blessed being is often depicted with lustrous black feathers in Angel calendars. This great being is much maligned and often referred to as "The grim reaper". Along with this nickname, there is always an inference that one must have done bad deeds to be taken by him.

Black is an earthly symbol for the absence of light so to see a dark angel we assume it is a "bad" angel. Perhaps we could shift our thinking and take the view that its blackness is a symbol of a persons/souls light going out on the Earth realms. This is the reason sensitive people are able to see a person with a black aura, and "know" that they are going to die soon. The black aura is indicating this person's purpose on Earth is completed for this time and space, and its time to return to the heavenly light realms.

My personal experience with this Angel of transition was one that filled me with wo*nder, awe and immense comfort. I was not afraid, and in fact I felt humbled that it had appeared to me. The shine on it's huge black wings was like polished coal*

and very, very, beautiful. This being was saying to me that I could pass on if I wanted to and that they would assist me in any way that they could, if that was my choice. This divine being then took me on a journey home to the light. At least I thought it was light until I got close enough to distinguish forms. I then found myself at a huge reception in what seemed like a ballroom. The air was filled with joy, love and golden light. WOW! This was amazing and so I asked,
"What is this celebration about? Who are we honouring?"
"You, our beloved sister, this is for your homecoming"
I was completely surrounded by gloriously dressed golden beings and there was heavenly music playing in the background. I do not remember staying or leaving, just the experience, because it transcended time and space. It was the most heavenly experience I have had so far this lifetime, and from that moment on I was a changed person. I no longer understood how anyone could be upset about the departure of a loved one. How could we be sad about a person going home to a reception such as I experienced. The answer is we could not be anything but happy for our precious loved one.

However, for the most part, here on Earth we make a souls leave taking, or death, a sad and sorrowful event. It is a sombre occasion, often filled with tears and even remorse over things not said or done.

Angels and light beings view this experience very differently. To them, it is the most joyous of occasions. This is because "One" of their own loving light beings is coming home. To the Angelic realms it is a time of celebration, love and happiness. It is a re-union, a chance and time to re-unite with many layers and levels of loved and beloved ones.
The universe is all the richer and blessed because they have returned to the Oneness, the Godhead, the cosmic consciousness and the Creator.

Feel the fear and do it anyway

Angels and Master Souls

The concepts of Master souls, or a higher Universal intelligence helping us as we travel life's highway, is not a new one. However it is believed that God, Source or the great I AM, created Angels, long before humans were added to the scheme of things.

The idea of this spiritual force from beyond the physical realm is to be found in every major religion or philosophy. Through the written word, tales, legends and mythology, the principal of worshipping, connecting or communicating with the gods, and spiritual forces is to be found in every culture and country in the world. This is not a nineteenth, a twentieth, or twenty first century phenomenon. Pictures of what we would call aliens today, have even been discovered in ancient caves as drawings, so primitive man knew there was a connection between them and the fifth dimension.

Throughout our history on Planet earth, human beings have understood the power of being connected to the higher forces in the universe. They should, as the universe is really their home, and where they truly belong. This powerful energy source has been called many things over the centuries such as,

Great Ancestors	Great White Spirit	Yahweh
Allah	Christ	The One
The Divine Creator	The All	God or The Gods

Ever since we, as spiritual beings, began to come to Planet Earth as part of our growth experience, we have always instinctively tuned into this force for help, answers, guidance, favours and blessings. At first we made this connection to the

Godhead or Goddess through nature and animal kingdom, by way of rocks, crystals, wood, bones, herbs and grasses, and totems.

Ancient man saw in himself the likeness to a particular animal or bird, and felt that the spiritual force within it could be called upon for guidance and protection. Soon it became clear that certain people could walk and talk with the gods much better than others, and so they were given a special place and title in the community. Thus began the Shaman, the person of healing and wisdom through which the gods spoke.

As races and cultures evolved, these "special" people were given titles such as medicine man/woman, witch doctor, witch, white witch, and more. As these community structures continued to evolve, religions and structures for worship emerged. Men of vision set these in motion because they saw a way that they could be the channels, or a medium through which the universe or god could pass on spiritual and universal truths to the masses.

These systems were initially designed to impart the "spiritual path" to its group, but along the way it became apparent that this was an amazing tool through which you could control people. From that point on the system, rituals, dogma, and theology became more important than the participants spiritual well being. God became the being with which you could make people feel guilty and fearful, and therefore bend them to your will. Left with choice of going to either heaven or hell, and no way of negotiating how you could change your path, people conformed and lost much of their personal and spiritual freedom.

By now the different religions had started to set themselves up as the only way to "The One God", so that they could achieve more power and control. At this time they began to set one faith at war with another. With the cry "My church is the only way to heaven" or "Ours is the One true faith" they began creating division between families, cities, and finally, nations.

Every now and then the Universe was able to send down a Spiritual Master or Teacher to keep the hope, truth and channels between earth and the heavens open. Masters such as Moses, Abraham, Buddha, Krishna, Mohamed, Christ, and Confucius came to earth to tell us that we could find a way to connect with God through many different avenues. Their coming taught us that we could choose one or many ways to do this. None were better than the other; each way was just an alternative route to reconnect with The All or One.

I love the story about the ascended masters being called into a conference to discuss and decide where the secrets of the universe should be hidden. Someone suggested that they should be hidden in the stars, so that only people who looked up would find them.
No! No! No! Was the consensus, because many people would be blind and then they would be discriminated against.
*Someone else suggested that they put the secrets in a large book, so that people would have to learn to read to find them. No! No! No! Was the cry. That would discriminate against those millions of beings who would never have the opportunity to be educated. Finally a master called out 'Why don't we put the **"secrets to life"** inside mankind, as it will be the last place he/she looks". **And so it was done.***

Meanwhile the Angels and Masters waited patiently for the right time and awareness levels to have the opportunity to connect with the masses. Well, that time has arrived. People all over Planet Earth are able to tap into these masters at will, providing that they can attune themselves to the highest energy vibrations possible. You see, the masters and Archangels cannot "lower themselves" to talk to us through the density of vibrations that surround earth, but will willingly meet us half way.

Because it is now possible to use methods to connect with Angelic realms, ordinary everyday people worldwide are experiencing visitations. Visions and messages from God and the universal Masters, similar to those recorded in the bible and ancient books, are becoming commonplace.

The heavens and galaxies are full of light beings, intelligent beings, ascended masters and star people, but the spiritual helpers we are most familiar with are called Angels, Guides, Spirit Guides or Great Ancestors. Angels have appeared in visions, dreams, and spoken to people as the messengers of god for centuries.

Although there is no way of proving the order of Angels, it is widely accepted to comprise of 3 hierarchies, with 3 levels in each.
1. Seraphim, Cherubim and Thrones
2. Dominions, Virtues and Powers
3. Principalities, Archangels and Angels.

Dominions oversee the energy of Countries and their role is the spiritual welfare of all its inhabitants. As a touring spiritual leader I have often seen and been spoken to by these great beings. They have often tested me to ensure that the values and principals I have are for the highest good of all concerned,

I was doing okay financially on my very first National workshop tour of Scotland, until I reached Glasgow. It seemed that no matter what I did I could not get a breakthrough on the radio, television, or the newspapers. I had had a fantastic interview with a journalist with the Glasgow Herald, only to be told that the story would not be published until long after I had left Scotland. However difficult it was, I was determined to follow my plan, as that was the commitment I had made to spirit.

With as much hope and faith as my dwindling financial resources could muster, I did the workshops (at a loss) and then moved on to Stirling. The day I arrived Irene Rose, a reporter from the Dundee Courier and Advertiser endeavoured to do a phone interview about my visit to Dundee. Three times we tried to get a clear telephone connection to do the interview on, to no avail. By this time the reporter was convinced it was not meant to happen.

I sent up a plea, please help me get a crystal clear telephone connection, or we will lose this opportunity, and I dialled up again. This time it worked and we spoke as if we were in the same room. This was very encouraging, because I felt as long as I could get to Dundee things would change for the better.

By now, financially I was down to £10.00, yes only £10.00. I went for a walk near Stirling Castle trying to live in the moment, and keep my faith that everything would be all right, but as I walked I started to weep.

I felt so down, alone and helpless, and was panicking about what on earth I could do change my circumstances. I looked for a retreat or place to hide because I was so embarrassed about my emotional condition. I found a church within a part of the walls around the castle, and went inside and sank into a pew under a stained glass window and broke into sobs.

I said" God I do not know what to do. I am doing our work and yet the burden is just too hard for me. I think you chose the wrong person for this mission, as I have not been able to make it work. I have enough money for my night's lodgings and then I will have none, what am I to do? Please help me".

I continued to cry, letting out all the tension in my body and mind.

As I gave in to the release of my fears, pain and surrendered to my helplessness, I saw and heard in my mind a man who was larger than life.

This divine Scotsman said in a strong clear firm voice "Shame on us Laddies, she has come to teach us independence and freedom, and we have let her do battle alone, shame on us". Then I saw a large number of clansmen *rise up from over glens and join the master soul I now know to be William Wallace. Then the vision faded and I sat there for another hour prolonging the moment I would have to leave this sanctuary and return to the day and my problems.*

To this day I have no clear recollection about the following five days, except that I had the money to lodge and feed myself, and move on to Dundee, for my next lot of public workshops. Where the money came from is a miracle in itself, as each time I had to pay for something the money was in my wallet.

As it turned out, the Dundee newspaper had published their story about my upcoming talks and workshops a week in advance. So! Imagine my surprise when I turned up people were queued up at the doors waiting to enter. So many people came I had to extend the room I had hired and ask the staff to find more chairs. Throughout the next two evenings I had well over 350 people attend my various programs, which meant my financial horrors were over.

As a footnote William Wallace came to me each day just to see if I was all right and to re-assure me that everything would be fine. I can still hear his lilting brogue saying "Dinna fach yerself lassie, dinna fash yerself". Many times, when I have returned to my beloved Scotland, I have felt this wonderful being's energy, strength and presence. William Wallace is connected to the large group of Principalities and Master Souls that oversee all things in Scotland.

Principalities look after Cities, Multi- National Corporations, Educational facilities and any very large structure involving people. They may also be seen and felt above:
- Prisons
- Hospitals
- War Zones
- Mental Hospitals
- Natural Disasters

In my travels around the world to different countries, I have had the privilege of seeing and working with the principalities. Many aware people all around the globe are called to help the masters at times of earthly crisis, such as wars, earthquakes, democratic upheavals, floods, and most recently, the September 11th disaster. These masterly "light workers" add their focused energy to help the Principalities and Archangels settle and heal the spiritual energy that has been disrupted in that area, or over that land mass.

One night in 1998, while I was living in London I, I sat down for a rest after work, before beginning to prepare my evening meal. I closed my eyes and was immediately swept from my body and found myself high in the sky over Ireland. I was surrounded by hundreds of light forms and Angels, and we were all forming a geometric dome over the country below us. We all had our arms raised above our heads forming a V shape, and our legs made the same V shape, and we were all connected together at our hands and feet. I felt we all looked like hundreds of Leonardo Davinci's Vetruvian man. It was a glowing living breathing grid of glistening white energy, and as we all inhaled together, we lifted the negativity and pressure off the situation. Then, as we exhaled, we spread the transmuted energy back out as pure high clear spiritual white light.
It was like being a leadlight windowpane in a huge universal widow that God was endeavouring to let light shine through. I was swept up in this experience for 10 days, and it ceased as suddenly as it began.
I now know that what I had been part of was a huge spiritual grid. This experience happened at the time that the Irish Government was negotiating, and ultimately signed, the basics of the Irish peace accord.

In my healing workshops we always include an astro trip to a hospital to join forces with the principalities or master Angels that are doing their healing works there. It is a wondrous experience to join up with this powerful healing force and go down into the wards with these angels and heal bones, surgical incisions, and assist at births. Also to be there to comfort those ready to pass on, or unite children who are feeling homesick, frightened and missing their parents, with their Angels.

I have always had an affinity with prisons, which must have come from past life times as I have had no personal experience with these institutions in this life. In my healing workshops, we also make time to astro travel to these institutions. The Principalities that oversee prisons are grateful to have our extra energy to assist them in their work. The energy is often so heavy and negative, that the extra boost of our being there makes the angels work easier.

I have always explained that the spiritual reason people are in prison is to stop them from accumulating more karma. These people are still spiritual beings with a team of spiritual helpers or angels helping them just the same as you and I. They are no lesser than us, it is simply that they have had different experiences which impacted on their lives, and therefore they have made different choices. Over the years I have put a lot of energy, healing, hope and unconditional love into prisons, as a spiritual community service.

In 1999 and 2000 I was experiencing excruciating back pain, so much so, that even lying down to go to sleep was agonizing. When I ended up in hospital, the doctors pumped me full of pain relief while they investigated the source of the problem. The specialists discovered I had a malignant tumour in my spine, so a course of treatment was embarked upon.
During my morphine induced stupor I had numerous visions, and visitations, but none so memorable as the following one.
I was in that strange state between sleep and being awake when two tall and large framed men appeared before me. They were quite frightening really, as they were completely

dressed in black. Black leather jackets, black tee shirts that one of the men had definitely outgrown, as it exposed a large part of his stomach, black leather pants and black motor bike boots. They had beards, were displaying tattoos and appeared very unkempt indeed. One of them said in a very gruff abrupt voice,
"Are you the Angel lady?"
To which I replied. "Yes, I suppose I am".
He continued, "Are you the Angel lady that visits the prisons?"
"Yes, I have taken astro trips to help the Angels who work with prisons" I replied.
"Well! We have been sent to tell you how much your visits have helped, and how much we appreciate what you do. That's all really, it was just to let you know that we do know what you do and it does help"
Then poof, they were gone. This was their way of returning a healing favour to me in my hour of need, and it still has a special place in my heart. It also served to reinforce to me that god will sometimes choose a very unlikely person to be an Angel when we are in need.

These Master souls, Higher beings, Teachers, Ancient Ones and Great Ancestors can be accessed by anyone who has the belief, intent and desire to do so. We all know that Sananda (Jesus Christ) is called upon or tapped into by millions of people in any given day. The same can be said for Mother Mary.

In 1978, when I was beginning to do talks and workshops on Spiritual matters, it was a new and courageous field to be entering. Unlike now, there were very few books on the subject, and you were definitely considered weird or to be viewed with a great deal of suspicion for talking about reincarnation, astro travel, Angels, auras and the like. I had been doing talks locally, and was still feeling a great lack of confidence, and uncertainty about the path that I was taking.

One night, just as I was going to sleep, a huge Angelic being appeared at the end of my bed. In hindsight it seemed to me to be 80 feet tall, a shimmering luminous metallic blue in colour, and was holding a lantern and a set of scales. It spoke not in words, but to my heart, and said that I was to continue on my path and that they would be asking me to go overseas with my message.
I was visited by that same huge Angel three more times, each time it appeared, it was prior to being asked to take my message oversees.
Many years later, the emphasis of my work shifted to past life healing and assisting people to balance out their karma. It was then that I came to understand that the glorious being I had seen was **Liberty,** *who is one of the seven divine Masters and Spiritual Lords of Karma. It was through the grace of these Lords of Karma that I was allowed to tap into the history of people I was counselling and help them heal issues that remained unresolved from the past.*

Archangels lead bands of angels, and oversee vast projects for the light or God source. While there are millions of Archangels throughout the universe, those mostly connected with earth are Michael, Gabriel, Raphael and Uriel. Only the first three of these are mentioned in the Bible. As angels are spiritual beings and therefore sexless, I am going to apply the most commonly used terms and refer to them as being of masculine gender.

Archangel Michael - whose name means "One who is like God" is often seen as a warrior angel carrying a sword. Michael is renowned for his valiant spirit of protective power, and is the being to call upon to fight an unfair cause for you, to cut ties with old experiences and relationships, and to move out or caste off obstacles or negativity. His retreat is said to be at Banff in Alberta Canada, and having experienced the fabulous energy there, personally, I am apt to believe it.

Archangel Gabriel is called the angel of the Annunciation, because it was he who informed Mary that she would conceive the Son of God. Gabriel is often depicted carrying lilies, as they symbolize purity. He also announced to Zacharias that he would have a son born to him who would be John the Baptist. It was Gabriel who inspired Joan of Arc to go to the aid of the king of France. In Islam, Archangel Gabriel, who dictated the Koran to Mohammed, heads the angel hierarchy. So you can see why he has gained the reputation for being a communicator.

If you can hold onto the idea that the source is the creator of all things, including movies, what better place to have the world centre of mass communication (Hollywood) than in California, because his retreat is said to be there at Mt Shasta. Gabriel's name means "hero of God" or "God is my strength".

Fatima in Portugal is said to be the place that **Archangel Raphael** has his retreat, and I can personally attest to the incredible amount of healing energy there. As I walked into the church I saw the blue healing energy filling the whole building. It was a place of deep rich calmness and serenity, the like of which I have never felt in a church before. He is often depicted as carrying the ancient symbol of healing, the fish and he is also called the angel of science and knowledge.

He is the most sociable of the Archangels, and is often funny, has the best sense of humour and the happiest disposition of all his peers. For this reason he is often depicted chatting merrily with mortal beings, and he delights in bringing health, happiness and joy everywhere he goes. Raphael has just said to me, Who would be better than Raphael to send down the saying; "A merry heart doeth good like medicine" or "Laughter is the best medicine".

Archangel Uriel is said to have given the Kabbalah, the Hebrew mystic tradition, to mankind.

Archangel Moroni facilitated the discovery of the divinely inscribed golden tablets that became the book of Mormon, and thus foundation of establishing the Mormon religion. Archangels Michael's, Raphael's, and Gabriel's energy source is so vast that we can all call on them and get our particular form of personal help at the same time and still there is energy to spare. These souls are too great to be one of your personal helpers, but at the same time they can be with you every day, and their help and energy can be felt worldwide. They will assist you with anything that you request of them, providing it is for your highest good.

People are also being visited by the following master beings, whom are at times, are identifying themselves by name. To this end they have requested that I include a list in alphabetical order, of the best known of them in this chapter. In doing so, they hope that you may recognize their name when they communicate with you to share their knowledge, insights, or wisdom.

Afra	Babaji
Buddha(Gautma Buddha)	Confuscious
Djwhal Khul	Elijah
El Morya	Ganesh
Hilarion	John the Baptist
Jesus(Sananda)	Kuthumi
Lanto	Maitreya
Maha Chohan	Mother Mary
Melchzedek	Metatron
Milarepa	Lady Nada
Paul(the Venetian)	Quan Yin
St Germain(Ragoczy)	Sanat Kumara
Sathya Sai Baba	Serapis Bey
Uriel	Zoroaster

While there are millions of Archangels throughout the universe, there are a small number that are well recognized here, and each has a particular area of interest and patronage on the earthly plane. They are as follows,

Archangel Michael	The patron angel of law and order and the military.
Archangel Gabriel	The patron angel of all who work in the field of communications
Archangel Raphael	The patron angel of all those in the field of medicine
Archangel Metatron	The patron angel of small children
Archangel Raziel	The patron angel of Law Makers
Archangel Sandalphon	The patron angel of Music
Archangel Israfel	The patron angel of Entertainers
Archangel Camael	The patron angel of all who love God
Archangel Jophiel	The patron angel of Artists
Archangel Azrael	The patron angel of The Clergy, and seen as the angel of death
Archangel Ariel	The patron angel of Wild Animals

You can make requests to any of these individual spiritual beings, or ask to be connected to a particular one for a specific purpose or length of time. Further more, you will have a natural spiritual link with some of them, almost as if you belong to their group, monad or family.

You will feel a natural affinity towards them, almost as if you "know" them, which indeed you do.

Now, in the twenty first century, the mass population on Planet Earth has increased its spiritual awareness to such an extent that it has altered earth's vibration. As people are individually becoming more enlightened and illuminated, it brings the overall vibration of the planet to a higher level. You do, and can, make a difference to the world we live in.

Evidence of this is seen in the countless numbers of people who do their spiritual work publicly, as in workshops, classes, talks and lectures, and our healers who are working with a wide variety of alternative, ancient and natural therapies. Our shaman, healers, white witches, psychics and visionaries from the past are here again, being open channels to and for universal consciousness.

We are moving beyond the physical focus in our lives, and seeking the higher way. A way in which all of us may be considered as one and our family will become the family of man. The ancient ones are restless to move on, but cannot do so until we, as a collective consciousness, move on to a higher plane.

The knowledge and wisdom about how this can be done is filtering down to innumerable people, who are being challenged to trust themselves and their inner guidance more than ever before. The September 11th disaster in New York, has taught us that nothing is truly safe or secure, and that all you can really rely on is your inner wisdom and your communication with spirit.

Today, as spiritual knowledge enlightens our modern world, we are re-connecting with not only Archangels, but also the Great Ones from belief systems other than that of Christianity. We have seen the resurgence of the Native American culture's wisdom, healing powers, and the benefits of some of their rituals. People's minds are also being opened to other sources of intelligence, such as universal entities from other Planets and time spaces.

Spirit will appear to you in forms that your mind and heart is open to accept. That is why some people see Angels, others see space beings, others see nature spirits, and others connect with creatures from the oceanic realms. This is the Creator or The All at work and it is simply many different forms of this huge pool of energy, each with its' wisdom to share. Every person on Planet earth has a form of spiritual guidance, whether your belief system has this as an angel, guide, teacher, ancestor, or a creature or facet of nature.

This force, which I will refer to as Angels or helpers from this point on, is committed to helping you be the greatest spiritual being you can be. Their role is to pass on direction, answers, suggestions, ideas and solutions to you about your life's journey. Unlike you, they do remember what it was you wanted to accomplish spiritually from your visit here.

If your life's purpose is best achieved by mixing and dealing with people, you will have three or more Angelic helpers in your team. Not because you are stupid, dumb or ineffectual and need extra help, but because working with people is more challenging, and you will need extra insights to be effective.

When you are moving into a new phase of life, dealing with a crisis, a new job, moving cities or countries you will get an extra team to assist your personal team of Angels. This extra help will give you more energy and protection until you are comfortable at the next level, at which time they will leave. If your Angels have to, they will even take upon a physical form to assist you in times of great need.

Judy, knowing I was teaching spiritual matters, confided in me one day that she had had a very unusual experience. Her husband and two sons all contracted the mumps at the same time. She was living in a new town so had no one she could call on for help. Taking care of the three of them alone was a huge task, and it was wearing her down. The cooking, changing the bed linen, doing the laundry and bed bathing everyone was taking it's toll and she was exhausted. She had gone two nights without sleep and in tears and desperation she called on God and her Mother for help.
Moments later, there was a knock at the door and when she opened the door there stood her Mother, who had passed on years before. Her mum said "I believe you need some help?" and then boldly walked through the door. She took charge, and sent my friend, to bed for a rest, and she assumed the responsibility of all the tasks at hand. For three days they

worked, cooked, talked and fellowshipped together as a team while they cared for the three males.
Judy said to me "Julia I never even questioned the fact that I knew Mum was dead, she was here and an answer to my prayers. It was wonderful to have her with me again". On the fourth day, it was apparent that the patients had all taken a turn for the better, and were able to do small things for themselves, thus alleviating the load that the women were bearing. With this her Mother went into the sitting room, and vanished.
Judy confided "Now you know why I have never told another living soul about my experience. They would just say that I was insane. Was it really my mother Julia? Could she come back like that?"
"Judy I cannot be certain if it was actually your Mum. It might have been or it could have been one of your angels taking on an acceptable form to you (the form of your Mum) in answer to your prayer.

Yes, you better believe it Angels can take up physical forms when necessary. I know, because it has happened to me at least twice. One of these experiences happened in 1979 in Berne, Switzerland and the other happened in 1998 Cairns, Australia.

I was visiting a very dear friend in Cairns, and as part of celebrating our being together we decided to go out for dinner, and we invited another friend to join us. As we were driving through town to find a car park near to the restaurant we had booked into for dinner, a young man came speeding through town and collided with us on my side of the car. Fortunately we were only doing 15 kilometres an hour, so the impact was not as serious as it could have been.
We all got out, much shaken, and took stock of the situation. It seemed that we were all unhurt, but in shock. The other two passengers went to survey the damage to both vehicles, which left me standing alone. In an instant a man was standing

beside me, asking me in the most beautiful voice, "Julia, are you alright?"

"I am fine" I replied,

"Are you sure you are alright?" He repeated. At which point I wondered if I had been hurt and was bleeding but had not noticed. I checked my body again, and No, I could see nothing amiss.

"Would you like me to ring the police?" he enquired.

"Yes" I said, "I think that would be a very sensible thing to do". At which he left.

Moments later he was back at my side.

"Julia, I rang the police, but they only have one patrol car on duty and it is busy, the sergeant at the watch wants to know could you all go around and report the accident to him at the police station".

It still had not dawned on me that a stranger was calling me by my first name. I turned to me friend Sharna, the driver of our car, and said.

"Sharna, this man has rung the police station and he says".... The look on her face made me stop.

"What? What is it?" I asked.

"What man Julia?" at which I turned to the man beside me and found that he had vanished. He was nowhere to be seen for 100 yards and he could not have walked away that quickly. Yet, he had vanished in to thin air.

"What was it that he said?" she asked.

"Well he said that the sergeant at the watch has only one patrol car on tonight, and it is busy. So he wants to know if we can drive to the [police station to report the accident".

We eventually drove to the police station, and as we all came through the door the sergeant at the watch said, "Oh good, you could make it, I told the man who rang to tell you about the patrol car being busy, I see he passed on my message okay".

Yes, one of my Angels, concerned for my well-being, had manifested as a human being and done earthly tasks to ensure my safety.

This is a classic example about how angels or master souls can transcend the spiritual – physical world, space and time to be earthly helpers when they are really needed. Sometimes people in physical bodies can be angels to us and these are commonly called White Angels. These are those wonderful people who make little miracles happen for you right when you need them the most. This is a special person who goes out of their way to assist you or be helpful by offering you a ride, assisting you when your car breaks down, or even giving you accommodation in their homes. White angels can come in the form of a doctor or nurse, a neighbour, a taxi or bus driver, a shop assistant, a child or teenager.

I remember a client of mine telling me about her son, when he was eight, asking her if she could pack an extra lunch for someone, but not ask him any questions about it. She duly did so, and it went on for months. Each day she made the extra lunch that her son took to school. One day he told her that he did not need the extra lunch any more as the person was okay now. It transpired many years later, that the unknown friend was a starving classmate and the extra lunch was his main source of food.
My client's son was being a white angel at the tender age of eight, and following a heavenly request to help his spiritual brother.

Master souls who guide us make no value judgments on our actions, for they know how valuable it is for us to have experienced something. This is how we gather our wisdom. Whether **WE** consider the outcome is:
Good or Bad   Right or Wrong   Perfect or Imperfect, our Angels see things simply as experiences. Above all things it is your intention that is the uppermost value. When the triangle of Intention, belief and desire are in alignment, your angels can assist in making the seemingly impossible take place.

Your Angels, Guides, or Helpers are ever present, they do not leave you, you actually tune them out. Imagine that you are a radio with several stations on the dial that you can choose to tune into. You may choose to spend a day tuned into mind talk, confusion, depression and self-criticizing commercials.

Or yet again, listen to the "expertise" and opinions of the many authority figures that are available to you every day. If you are willing, any number of well meaning teachers, parents, relatives, colleagues, accountants, bank managers, tutors and professionals will proceed to tell you what to do or what they think is best for you.

However you can choose to tune into the fifth dimension and beyond, where the Angels and masters hang out. Their commercials are really great and confidence boosting, the music or sounds are harmonious and uplifting to your energy levels, and they are the best cheerleaders in the land for you and what you desire to do.

**An Angel is just like everyone else,
only more so**

Your Personal team of Angels and Helpers

Everyone has an Angel, Guide or Helper; yes, even you. In fact you may have more than one and this depends on what you came to Planet Earth to do or achieve. If your life purpose is to do with interacting and being of service to people, you will have three or more in your team. Conversely, if your plan is to do with the making, creating, or working with "things" you will have one or two angels to assist you.

This "personal" team will be with you for the whole of this life's journey. They are the mainstay of your connection with the Godhead, The All, or The Oneness. Your Angels have been with you since before you were born, and will stay with you until after you pass on, pass over or die.
So what are angels or Guides or helpers? They are evolved forms of love, light and wisdom – expressions or messengers of God and the universe. But who are they? Well, **"In heaven an angel is nobody in particular"**

Helpers, Guides and Angels are beings that have mastered all the wondrous experiences here on planet earth. Such as being

Rich – Poor	Ill – Healthy
Warrior – Helpless	Man - Woman
Child - Very old	Compassionate - Callous
Benevolent - Self centred	Master - Slave and so on.

While taking on theses roles they practised the actual living of the universal spiritual laws. They did this repeatedly until they reached that state of being known as love. Then, one of their options is to help and encourage us into the same state of awareness. They too, will continue learn and grow from their opportunity to assist you.

So lets review the big picture and start at the beginning. Firstly you are a soul or spiritual being or energy. You don't have a soul – you are one.
Your true home is called many things like heaven, god, the all, the now, the universe, paradise, the garden of Eden, nirvana, the cosmos, I Am consciousness, and the Creator, depending on your belief systems.

This is where we belong, we always did and we always will. Together we are all just visiting planet earth to "experience" life and practise living the universal laws. As souls we actually "know" all there is to know, so we come here to earth to experience living what we know.

It is a huge spiritual adventure in living and experiencing all the amazing opportunities and things we can do here. For example, things like,
- Exercising our free will
- Creating our own life experiences
- Making manifest our own thoughts
- Manifesting our goals and dreams
- Making decisions
- Being empowered or disempowered

So there you are, a soul, out there in the universe, thinking about what you would like to experience next. Taking time to consider what would be exciting, motivating and worthwhile to you and that would ensure your continuing journey towards oneness. When you have decided, you then ask for help and expertise to achieve your dreams, goals and spiritual growth. This way you know you will return to earth fully equipped with all the answers available to you for any of the experiences you will encounter.

At this point a team of angels, guides, spirit guides, helpers, teacher, masters, great ancestors, ancient ones, wise ones, whatever you choose to call them, will offer their wisdom to assist you in your purpose.

Because you chose or organised your angelic team of wise ones before you were born, it means that anyone who has been on the planet at the same time as you, can't be an angel or guide for you. They may be around you, however they are not part of your angelic/light being wisdom team.

That is: your mother, father, grandmother, brother or aunt cannot be your one of your guides or angels. Once they have passed on and given us time to grieve, they need, and want, to move on and to continue their growth process. Often we can unknowingly hold them back, by not being willing to let them go. Letting go is one of life's major growth experiences, and we need to "let go" of people and things so we can move on to the next level in life.

As your angels don't have physical forms, they can't talk to you through physical forms of communication. Instead they use the language of the soul – the spiritual language of symbols, feelings, intuitions and sensitivity is also known as the psychic gifts. (These four gifts or means of communication are covered in depth in subsequent chapters)

Your angels have come to help you be the very best YOU, you can be. They have been inspiring, helping, guiding and loving you, your whole life. They love you so unconditionally, therefore they see nothing you do, or have ever done as:
Right or Wrong   Good or Bad   Should or Shouldn't
It is you, with your belief systems, who colour it with your value judgements, because to your Angels, everything is "just an experience". If you can process and internalise this idea, it will revolutionize your relationship between yourself and

your angels. Why? Because you will no longer have the need to judge yourself for the decisions, actions and choices you have made.

Your angels would rather you brought to them your dreams and longings of the soul, for in focusing on your desires and dreams of the heart, most of your troubles would vanish. When you focus on your troubles the universe will stand aside and allow you the freedom to do so, for they cannot assist you while you are in this state of mind. However, the moment you focus on what you truly want, and start the intentions of changing your thoughts, attitudes and circumstances, you are co-creating with the universe and all the heavenly beings will be their to assist you.

At one point in my life I was feeling so low, for it appeared that I would need to enter bankruptcy. I felt guilty, bad, a failure, untrustworthy etc, because people had entrusted me with loans that it seemed I would not be able to repay. When I had calmed down, my angels said that "Having no money is not bad, nor is having lots of money good, they are just different experiences needing different solutions or approaches". They then proceeded to give me solutions and ideas to use to change my circumstances, and in no time at all my financial situation had changed dramatically.

Your angels will always give you at least three alarms that a particular course of action is not beneficial. Should you choose not to listen, you will find yourself in an uncomfortable, unpleasant or undesirable situation. This may result in you wasting valuable time, money and energy. When your angels are talking or communicating with you, you will sense it as:

    Always uplifting.
    Filling you with the confidence to act.
    A feeling like a piece of the puzzle has fallen into place.
    A feeling of expansion in your energy.

A heightened understanding.
Moving you into or onto bigger, larger and more challenging things.
Helping you see what you have learned or gained from situations.
Showing you how to be a better you.
Giving glimpses weeks, months or even years ahead.
Showing you things you are capable of.
A feeling to trust in yourself and your instincts

So let me tell you some "Angel" stories, to illustrate some of these points.

I remember driving home from a workshop late at night, and I was tired. I had been offered accommodation but I chose to push on home instead, even though the drive was 2 hours long. I drove through a small town and in the dim light, misread the signpost, so I ended up on the wrong road. I was doing 120 kilometres when the tar sealed road suddenly ended and it became a shingle road. My car went out of control and was veering and spinning in the loose stones.
At this point I took my hands and feet off all the car controls and prayed. "I guess this is it" I said, "I'm coming up Angels". All at once I felt someone's hands on my wrists guiding them back to a holding position on the steering wheel and hands under my knee joints guiding my legs up and down on the clutch, accelerator and the brake.
The next thing I knew I was parked, as if I was at a city kerbside parking meter, on the side of the road. I can tell you I drove the rest of the way home at 50 kilometres an hour, clinging desperately to the steering wheel. When I arrived home my anxious husband rushed out to the car to meet me. "Are you alright? I was worried about you. You look like you have seen a ghost" "I have" I said, "I think it was my own"

Your angels are always watching over you, and yes! Whenever necessary, they will protect you. However, there are much more fun things they would rather be attending too on your behalf, if they were given your permission. .

It was like the story of the lady driving up the Bombay Hills, and as she neared the top and was gathering speed, she decided to change from 2nd gear to 3rd gear, but the gearshift was jammed. She tried again with the same result; the gearshift was still jammed.
She figured that the gearbox was damaged and accepted that it would be a very slow drive in 2nd gear all the way to her destination.
When she drove over the brow of the hill, there before her, was a six- car pile up, with vehicles scattered everywhere. As she drove past slowly, once again she tried to change gears again and this time it worked. You see her angels had protected her from being the 7th car in the accident by forcing her to drive slowly in $2n^d$ gear, until she was safely over the brow of the hill and past the accident zone.

I am always amused when I hear the unemployment statistics of any country or city I am visiting, because people being out of work is such a concern for our society. I can appreciate these statistics, however, from my point of view "heavenly unemployment" is at disastrous levels. Our angels and guides are so often left with very little to do because we do not use, or ask for their assistance anywhere near enough.

Most of us will call out for help to God – Jesus – or the universe when we are stuck, or in need. Others will use their angels to get them convenient car parks and there is absolutely nothing wrong with these requests. However there is so much more that your team could be assisting you with if you had a bigger picture of your life.

Put yourself in your Angels shoes for a moment. There you are, with all the power of the universe at your disposal, should you need it. You and your other angel associates are all set to accomplish unbelievable successes and miracles in a particular persons life. You are all waiting for the first dream, or goal to be decided upon so that you can all move into action, and you here a plaintive cry. You are all filled with a rush of energy and excitement as you all prepare for action and you finally hear the request. "Find me a parking space please?"

I do not mean to diminish the task of an angel to find you a very convenient place to park your car. It's just that they would love to be doing so much more in your life.

Your angels want the joy of being able to help you, forward focus on things like:
    Education
    Having fun leisure and holidays
    Monetary affairs
    Your career path
    Your health and your healing abilities
    Unfolding your potential
    Expanding our spiritual knowledge
    And rising above our limitations
    Your personal leadership skills
    How you can be of service to people, the community and planet
    Family and/or personal relationships

Our angels long to help us see how far we could go in life, and to do the things that we are passionate about; Like living our dreams.

I'm a classic example. I was raised in a very poor family, and left school at the age of 15, with the assessment that I could be a factory worker or shop assistant. I could never have fantasised at the age of 20 or even 35 that my life would be where it is today. I had toyed around with the idea of writing a book for a few years, and even got as far as writing 4 chapters on one theme, but there seemed no impetus to continue, so I gave up.

One night my Angels woke me up at 2.30am and kept repeating the same words over and over in my head "write a book and write it like a dictionary." When I heard these words it was if a complete understanding or knowing flooded my head and I knew exactly what to do, even though I still doubted my ability to action the idea.

So the next day, with more faith than skill, my pen was put to paper, and I began to write my first book long hand. People proceeded to tell me that I could not possibly write a book without a computer. At first, I really bought into people's well-meaning criticisms and felt discouraged and crestfallen.

However, my angels continued to encourage me to proceed and write my chapters longhand. They reminded me, with a touch of wry mirth, the "Old Willy Shakespeare didn't have a computer and his plays have done okay". This was the motivating force I needed. After a while, if people made comments about my writing a book by hand, my quick reply was "Hey! Old Willy Shakespeare didn't have a computer and he did okay".

Anyway, a chapter at a time, week by week the book was written. Then I had a manuscript that needed typing, editing, proofreading and printing. A step at a time my angels brought me the right people to accomplish and complete each process. The end result was my first book. The point to this story is that your angels will always give you the inspiration to get started on something, but they may not give you all the details. However, when you do get started, the steps will be revealed.

A great part of working with spirit is trusting that you will know what you need to know, when you need to know it. I think this is a good definition of trust or faith. Just do it – a step at a time – and in no time at all it will all unfold as it should and the project will be completed.

Eighteen months previously, the idea of writing a book, any book, was a fantasy. As time has revealed, it was only one of five in print and the outline of number six is on the drawing board.

Your angels will sow the seeds of things you are capable of doing, or what you could achieve or become, weeks, months or even years ahead. Then, when the right place, time and people synchronise, the seed will grow into a tree. What they will show you are choices, options and possible outcomes, based on your skills, innate talents, direction and potential as a soul.

My dear sister Glenis is another perfect example of being in the right place to unfold latent talents. At one point in her life she was unemployed and wanted to re enter the work force. She applied for, and got a job doing computer office work, which I will say she is very skilled at.
However, right from day one, it was apparent to her that it was not working out. The previous staff member had been there 6 years and had devised systems that worked for her, but that made no sense from an efficient and logical business point of view. Glenis put herself under extreme pressure to try and make the situation work, but in the end she gave in after 2 weeks and left.
A few days later her sister in law suggested she apply for a job at a nursing home where she worked, because they were looking for more staff to care for the elderly. Glenis applied for the job, was accepted and started work that same week. She just loves the work and has endless patience for her elderly charges, treating them with dignity, respect and simple human kindness. She has been a carer now for three years and is in love with her work more today than ever.
By the way, my sister has a background of driving buses, trucks, skippering a 56foot yacht, running businesses, and being a highly adventurous woman indeed. Never could we, as her family, have guessed that there was this divine skill to care for elderly people hidden away inside her, just waiting for an opportunity to shine forth.

Let me say here, it is "your life" your free will and your choice, and what will become of it, is up to you. It is your destiny, your canvas to paint, your tapestry to weave with rich colours, textures and hues, and your ship to captain and steer. No one can be born for you and no one can die for you, and what ever happens in your life is up to you. So don't look for your angels to "tell you what to do", because that's what earthlings do, not angels.

You see, its not what happens to you in life that is of great account, but what you do, or how you deal with it, or what you make of it, that gets written in your history book. There is no limit to what they can do on your behalf. Having said that, you must do your share. You can't sit on the sofa making demands and expect to get it all handed to you on a plate. When your actions or deeds match your thoughts and intentions, this is the meeting place of magical events and outcomes.

When you angels come close to you, you may experience that: Someone good is watching over you.
        Or feel very protected
        Or feel surrounded by love
        Or have warm loving feelings
        Or get that chilly, goose bump sensation

This is caused because angels have a very high vibration of energy. When they come in contact with your or energy field, you get a shock, which is felt by your nervous system. This ricochets through your body as goose bumps, or that shivery chilly feeling that runs down your spine or your arms and legs.

Your angels want you to know that no matter how old you get, it is okay to be scared about new things.
In fact it's quite logical. Think about it, if you have never experienced something, then you have no frame or reference

to draw on to give you confidence. The secret is to be scared, but do it anyway.

If you can imagine that symbolically you are a donut. That tiny hole in the centre is (the past) your weaknesses such as, anger – guilt's – fears – resentments etc. As long as you focus on these emotions, or things and qualities that you don't have, your angels are almost powerless to help you, as the past can't be changed. Your past is simply a series of experiences that you are meant to, or have, gained wisdom from.

Your angels want you to focus on the donut (the present) and work with what you are good at by accentuating your positives. The universe does not want perfect people, it wants and prefers people who are continually willing to make the best of what they have.

The emphasis of Spiritual growth has changed from the eighties and nineties, which was when the focus was on clearing out blockages, issues, therapy and counselling. Of course there will always be a place for these forms of self-discovery, however the new millennium is all about focusing on your strengths, skills and the things you're good at, and forgetting the rest.

I am not skilled with technology, and in this area I resist new things with a passion. I am always scared I will break something, cause a disaster, or even worse, find out I am not bright enough to operate the equipment. This fear has lead my very slowly into the world of computers. I have to say now that I own one, I do not know how I did so much without it.
My point however, is that I am here to communicate with people, not be a computer wiz. If a computer task is too difficult or time consuming for me, I prefer to pay someone else to do it for me, allowing them to use their skills, while I get on with what I am good at.

Here are two more examples of people who became legends in their own time, despite their weaknesses.

Mother Theresa had a difficult path within the church because she was a rebel and was inspired by a vision quest. For all this, she went on to be a living saint as she followed her calling to allow even the poorest people to die with dignity. Princess Diana (it was stated) was bulimic, a self-mutilator, suffered from severe self esteem problems, and yet became an amazing example of a beautiful, deeply compassionate human being. She cared deeply about the plight of her spiritual brothers and sisters, regardless of their illness, race, age, financial circumstances, culture and customs. She was also a divine example of universal love in action, showing it by her deeds.

Apart from attending to your spiritual growth, your Angels love to have fun and pleasure with you.
I had been considering taking a holiday. I had three different destinations to choose from and I had asked my angels for a sign to let me know which one would be for my highest good at this time.
So there I was, presenting an Angels workshop in Christchurch where we were all giving and receiving of messages for each other. As the group was an uneven number I was paired up with a young woman, who by the way, thought she was a real novice student.
She took my hand and said "Your angels love working with you, because they have so much fun, and they especially love taking holidays with you".
Do you know, up until this message, I had never considered that a vacation was also an important spiritual experience. I had not realised that it is a time for the re-creation of energy, vitality, and mental and emotional pleasure. I suppose it is not called "recreation" or re-creation for nothing.

Another woman I met in New Plymouth told me she was thinking of moving to Australia, and that she had asked her angels to give her a sign. Later that week, while she was out "lunching", three times a bus drove past with A.N.S.E.T.T. Australia (an Australian airline) advertising signs all over it. So I asked "Well! Are you going?" her reply was "I'm still not sure." Illustrating to me once again, that your angels can suggest or guide you, but it is your life, your body and your free will.

Your angels are like a group of cheerleaders encouraging you ever onwards, and into better and more spiritually appropriate situations. Their messages ring out with optimism and encouragement, saying;
  Go for it, you can do it.
  You did fantastically well.
  We are proud of you and your efforts.
  Have courage, proceed, we are with you every step
  of the way.
  You deserve to have the fullest measure of happiness.
  We love and accept who you are.
Aspire to trusting yourself more because you "do know" what is right for you, as they urge you ever onwards and upwards onto bigger and brighter horizons.

Your angels love to help you help yourself and to find the right answers and be a catalyst for finding the perfect solutions to situations. They will help you heal yourself by assisting, guiding or leading you to find: The right doctor, alternative therapies, the right book, or show you ways to correct, improve or change your views or attitudes. They will also channel healing energy to you day and night if and when you need it.

No matter how Dark your Darkest hour is, your angels are always with you, waiting for you to ask for their help and divine intervention. They love to enjoy and be a part of the process of living, loving, understanding and sharing with you and through you. Their mission is to assist you to be the most "divine" expression of the God energy that you can possibly be.

To this end, they can, and indeed will, move heaven and earth to bring this into being. Talk to them, confide in them, and share both your tears and laughter with them. Walk with courage in your actions and hope in your heart and you will indeed be lifted up on the wings of angels.

Hark the herald Angels sing

How you can use your Angels more.

Angels, please help me to stay organised.
You can request help in special areas of your life. When I am in a particularly busy business period, with lots of projects on the go, I ask for some help from my angels to help me stay on top of things.
They will assume the role as my personal organisers and send me prompters or reminders about, paying bills on time, phone calls to be made, appointments to be kept and dry cleaning to collect.

Angels, have I got all I need for this day or trip or appointment?
I use the following technique a lot, and it can save me a great amount of time and frustration. Before I leave home I stand at the unlocked front door and ask, "Okay angels have we got everything we need for this trip?" then I take a deep breath let it out and listen. So often I am reminded of something that I have forgotten to pack like,
a diary   Slides   Keys   Purse   Laundry   A raincoat   or mail that I need to post. Having collected the item I ask the question again and then listen.
If all is quiet I leave.

I remember leaving my friends home in Christchurch and my angels gave me a strong feeling to return to the bedroom I had slept in. I ignored the message, as I had already done a second check to see if I had all my belongings and that I had left nothing behind. Admittedly I did not enter the bedroom, but just glanced around the room while I stood in the doorway. I got 15 kilometres away when my mobile phone rang, and yes, I had left hanging clothes in the wardrobe. I never noticed them from the doorway, because the wardrobe door was open and it obscured my view. Had I entered the room properly, I would have seen my clothes immediately.

Angels, I need a person/persons to assist me.

Sometimes I have requested that my Angels find me the most appropriate person to help me at my workshops, doing my banking, driving or collecting me from hospital, attend to my mail, do my housework when I was too sick to do so and the like. These wonderful people are like heaven sent Angels, always arriving at the very time I need them.

Angels, can you help me with my Business affairs?

Over the years I am amazed at the help that has come from my angels about business matters. I have told my angels about the specific help I need and it's quite awesome to see how my requests have manifested themselves.

For example:

In the year 2000 I asked my angels for some new merchandising ideas, as I wanted to expand my services so I could reach more people. Thereby moving closer to fulfilment of my life mission, which is to make a huge positive difference to our world. Well that simple request has resulted in "chance" meetings with people who freely gave me their time and knowledge about:

    Expanding my product range
    Branding
    Upgrading my market image
    Improving customer services
    Training others to do what I do
    Countries I would work in
    Key contacts in various countries
    All of which came to me for no fee at all.

Angels, please help me Purchase a new car

For the last 30 years I have always bought cars by following my Angels recommendations, and been truly blessed by purchasing reliable, efficient, low maintenance vehicles. Here's my formula. I decide how much I have to spend or invest in a car. I then ask for their help to find a vehicle that will be reliable and need no major mechanical repairs for the time I own it. This time stipulation has varied from six months to three years. I commit to maintaining the vehicle by doing things like replacing or repairing, brakes, tyres, clutch, battery etc.

I then tell them when I want to buy it, for example Saturday week, or in the week of $10^{th} - 17^{th}$ June and after that I follow my feelings, hunches and intuitions. I have bought cars from newspaper, car lots, and car auctions, and in every case my perfect car was like a huge magnet drawing me to it. It drew me to the right advertisement or the right car sales yard, so that I find it.

One car was bought at an auction, and it was certainly not the car I would have selected. I wanted a sleek sporty job that looked a bit impressive. But, while wandering around looking and considering various vehicles, at three different times, three different men appeared at my side, and asked me what I was looking for.
I told them my price bracket and criteria, at which each of these wonderful men pointed to the same vehicle and said "That car over there is the best buy in your price range."
The car was non-descript white four-door sedan that I had not even given a glance. Needless to say I bought it. Why? because my angels will always give me three signs to indicate a particular direction, choice or decision. However it was quite a scary process, as my money was "gone"(in the speed of the auction process) in less than two minutes. I travelled the length and breadth of New Zealand in it, and she was a truly wonderful vehicle.

Having fun with your Angels
I love using my angels as social companions and fun executives. As I spend so much time travelling on my own, we have developed a great ability to have fun and enjoy life together. When I need a "mind shift", a healing, a pick me up, or need to switch off, I give them the chance to choose the movie that we would all enjoy. The result is,
- They show me the funny side of life.
- Being re-energised from being in peels of laughter.
- Helping me understand people and life better.
- Getting in touch with my feelings when I've been too much in my head.
- Educating me.
- Stimulating me to think about something in a different light.

The result is often a tear soaked handkerchief when a movie has really touched my soul. After these experiences it has sometimes taken me several minutes to "return to the present". This is because they helped me to have such a revitalising and complete mental vacation in a short 2-3 hours. I had "switched off and let go" of the world and all it's demands for a brief time and therefore completely rejuvenated my energy levels.

Angelic help shopping and getting bargains.
Your angels love to shower you with prosperity and bring the riches of the universe into your life. My greatest angelic game is finding bargains, not any old bargains, but items that I have decided I need or want, and I enlist their help to find the perfect item. I feel it is important to state that I am willing to pay full price, whatever that may be - $50 or $500. Having declared the willingness to do so, I rarely have to pay full price for my chosen items. I will find the perfect item given to me, second-hand, on sale or at a special price. Its so exciting, and such a thrill, to be blessed

this way, and of course it makes my finances stretch even further.

Resolving Relationship difficulties
If you are having what appear to be irreconcilable difficulties with another person, you can ask your Angels to collaborate with the other person's Angels to find a resolution. This is particularly helpful technique to use with work and business associates. It does not automatically mean that you will "win" or get your own way. If you use this technique you must be very open about the kind of solution that will come forth.

Sometimes it means that you will get another job; or the other person leaves because of ill health; or they retire to look after a sick/elderly relative. However, you can rest assured that if you sincerely make this request of your Angels, a solution that is for the highest good of both parties will come forth.

I hope this has given you an overview of ideas on how you can use your angels in a variety of ways in your everyday life. Your angels love to help you and willingly lend a hand in enabling you to live a happy relatively stress free life.
By assisting you with your day to day affairs, it will give them more opportunity to move you into a bigger picture, about what you can achieve and become. It is such a joy to them to help you be more creative in your approach to life. Being creative is simply finding:
> New ways to do things
> New ideas to implement
> New views or perspectives to see life from
> New approaches to situations,
> all of which is very exciting and energising.

Put your angels to work and dare to ask for help with:
- Business ideas
- Money matters
- Communication concerns

- Holidays
- Hobbies & Leisure
- Further education
- Past life information
- Relationship matters

Remember, they are unemployed until you decide what you want from life and ask for their help to achieve the goal. Whatever it is, don't forget the old adage:

***Ask and it will be given to you
Seek and ye shall find
Knock and the door will be opened***

If you do your share towards creating the life you desire, the universe will rearrange itself to accommodate your wishes, hopes and dreams. When your belief, intention and desire, are all in balance and focused towards a particular goal, it will materialise so quickly it will be breathtaking. This is when you manifest things as if by magic.

**Angels can fly
because they take themselves lightly**

The Language of Angels

The language of spirit, angels, God or the universe has been known in every culture, race, philosophy, religion, since ancient times. Every human being through time immemorial has been able to communicate with the heavens. The basis of all spiritual communication is telepathic using the same as the airwaves that are used for many forms of communication today.

For centuries this communication with the heavens has guided individuals, yet history records only the "Special" people with this connection to the gods like, Josef, Joan of Arc, Abraham, Moses, Mozart and Leonardo de Vinci to name but a few.

People who had this connection with the heavens were often elevated into positions of power, given titles and great wealth. Over centuries, priests, priestess's, and holy men perpetuated this myth. The commoners and masses were slowly led to believe that only these elevated people could communicate with God. If you were able to receive messages from the world of spirit, and you were not part of the church or establishment, then you were seen as a threat and punished accordingly.

If you are reading this book, then it is highly likely that you have been persecuted for your gift of being able to connect with the fifth dimension and the heavenly realms. It is true; you have to be an elevated person to connect with Angels; elevated in your thoughts, feelings, and energy only; which has nothing to do with your station or position in life.

When you attune yourself by chanting, praying, meditating, singing, being happy, spiritual cleansing, or surrounding yourself in peace, calm and white light, your energy is raised into the same vibration as the light and angelic realms. This creates and opens the perfect energy connection with the universal realms and a wavelength along which communication can travel.

Your angels have such a strong desire for you to recognise the messages they send, that they will repeat them several times in the hope that you will pick them up. Their commitment to you is to help you rediscover how "great" you really are and to;
1   Help you find out just how far you can go with any given opportunity, path, or chosen pursuit.
2   Encourage you to exercise your choices and free will, and to follow your dreams and inspirations.
3   Stretch the sides, or move out of the "box", group, culture, religion or society in which you were raised and to experience a limitless adventure here on planet earth.

Planet earth has many restrictions, limits and beliefs that society imposes on us, thereby influencing our power to exercise our choices, opportunities and achieve our long felt dreams. Spiritually, there are no such limitations or restrictions, you are never too old, dumb, young, uneducated, or any other of societies constraints to do, or become, anything you truly desire.

On Planet earth you can comply with all its restrictions and become a master of limitations, or you can choose the spiritual super highway to the super awareness consciousness and rejoice in its unlimited freedom while you are here. The choice is ultimately yours. Helping you to unfold your greatness and unlimited potential is the primary task of your team of angels. Each day they send you messages, answers, insights, hints and direction, but you are the one who has to be open to receiving these heavenly communications.

There is a wonderful saying about our communication with our angels.
Angels are speaking to all of us – Some of us are just better at listening.

Your spiritual sensory system is constantly receiving information about the world around you. I call this your spiritual alarm system because it is always giving you feed back about things to proceed with or things/situations to be cautious about. This is what people refer to as intuition or being psychic. I can almost hear you saying "But I'm not psychic!" Well let me tell you some of the most common psychic experiences that people have and see if you recognise any of them:

Hearing your name called and no one is there.
Having that strange de já vu (I've been here before) sensation.
Thinking of someone and they telephone you.
Following a gut instinct or intuition and it was correct.
Hearing that someone's "intention" does not match his or her words or declarations.
Writing screeds and screeds in letters/stories or journals effortlessly.
Thinking something and someone else says it.
Sensing the feelings or vibes from houses, restaurants, or shops.
Having an imaginary playmate.
Having a night time dream come true.
Knowing the right time to act.
Having healing hands or a green thumb.
Having an affinity to animals.
Seeing "energy" around things or people.
Seeing a soul or person who has passed on.
Picking up someone else's pains or illness.

The word psychic derives from the Greek word psyche – which means: Breath of the Soul   Breath of God
Yes! I will agree that some people have unfolded their abilities to amazing degrees, but that should not make you undermine your own skills. As yet, I have not been able to predict major disasters, global catastrophes or world trends and that's because its not what I came to do. You do have the skills and abilities to get all the answers you will ever need for your life, so don't get caught up in comparing your skills with anyone else's.

I feel the real question is "Are you listening?" or do you ask for God or Angelic help and then not tune in for their answers? To receive messages from the universe you need to make time to listen. That time can be in the form of meditation, gardening, relaxing in the bath, driving the car, time alone in your room, or drinking a cup of tea out in the peacefulness of the garden. The fifth dimension and beyond has a vibration of peace and stillness, so to receive your answers you need to create a similar vibration within yourself

Your angels will send messages and confirmation about a course of action through signs and symbols. They will use:
Television   movies   newspapers   books
people   animals   clouds   dreams
radio   songs   signs in nature feathers
in fact, anything at all, as a symbol to tell you something.

In Scotland they are fond of saying "It's a sign, it's a sign", if they get a second reference to something, for they understand that this is a message from the universe. I have to say, I use this method a lot myself. If I am thinking of doing something, and a part of me is uncertain, unsure, or needs the confidence to take a particular action, I ask for a sign.
I want the sign to confirm what I'm doing is for the greatest or highest good.

Then when I get the sign, and I assure you its unmistakable, it gives me the extra confidence to act.

When your angels want to communicate with you they do so through your, heart, feelings, unconscious mind or sensitivity. It is in this part of you that all your answers, skills, talents, wisdom and potential lies. This is your powerhouse of energy and drive, and the source of your passion and enthusiasm for life. They will ignite a spark of inspiration in your feelings with an idea, thought, image, or inner knowing, which will give you a rush of energy, excitement and a desire to act.

At this point you will often find yourself saying "But" and then beginning an endless stream of mind talk which will tell you why you could not, or should not, proceed with the idea. Your conditioning from our societies collective consciousness will assert itself and give you as many valid reasons or justifications as you want, for not following your inspiration. Whenever you are torn between following your head or your heart and inspiration, the guideline is, choose your heart or feelings. Have the courage to follow your spirit without hesitation.

The messages you receive from your angels can come at any time of the day or night. They may even wake you up at 3-4am to talk to you or to give you a message. I teach people in my night classes to have a pad and pen beside their bed for just such an occasion. Many of them have received tremendously inspirational messages through automatic or creative writing at this quiet hour of the morning.

Some time ago I was interviewing people for a position of trust. This new staff member would be in charge of considerable amounts of cash, and for the main part, work unsupervised.
My business partner and I were interviewing the applicants together, so that we could agree on the appropriate person to

employ. One of the applicants opening statement was that he had just been released from prison for theft as a servant. He went on to explain and if we did not know what that mean; it meant that he had stolen money from the cash register. He said he felt his beautiful wife and sons deserved a better life. He vowed that he had learnt from his experiences, and he wanted us to give him a 2nd chance.

My feelings told me he was being very sincere and honest, and that he would be trustworthy if we gave him the opportunity. My partner was a very intellectual person and not very compassionate or understanding about people who have made "Mistakes" with their lives. Well, as you can imagine, his head was flooded with common thoughts like:
> Once a thief, always a thief.
> A leopard can't change its spots.
> We are asking for trouble etc.
> He's a proven criminal.
> He cannot be trusted around money.

We discussed all the applicants, and my sensitivity still told me to hire this particular man, but my partner would not agree to do so. That night my angels woke me up from a deep sleep and said to me "take him on – he will be the best investment you ever made."

In the morning I told my partner about the message I received from my angels, and that I wanted to follow their suggestion. Begrudgingly he said, "So be it, do what you want, but the moment there is money missing from the cash drawer he gets fired".

So, because my Angels were so insistent, I hired the man, and he turned out to be the most loyal, honest, diligent staff member I have ever had the pleasure to employ. What's more, he was responsible for increasing our turnover immensely because of his natural people skills.

You have always had the ability to receive communication from your angels. In our society it is often seen as woman's intuition and therefore a weak or unsubstantiated nonsense.

That being so, men may refer to it as "gut instinct". The language of angels can be categorised into four main methods, and you have the ability to receive messages through all four channels or methods.

Do you recall that I described your physical body as being like a rental car? Well the four spiritual forms of communication are like its four speed gearbox. You can use all four, yet one of them is your first gear, because it is the most natural way for you to receive your angel's messages through.

Over time you have developed a great ability to use this particular form of perception, creating a greater sense of self-trust when you receive messages in this manner. It is important to unfold all four forms of the spiritual language within yourself, if you want the strongest connection with the highest of heavenly and universal realms.

**A guardian Angel 0'er his life presiding
Doubling his pleasures, and his cares dividing.**

Prophecy

The first language I want to cover is the gift of prophecy. The universe runs on this gift, which is why all spiritual books say that "you know" everything. The frustration about this statement is that we have all passed through the memory of forgetfulness and so now we have to re-member that which we already know.

This facet of your spiritual communication is always scanning the future, as it wants to know what will happen and how things will turn out. This is the part of you that sends you off to clairvoyants and psychics for a reading. You yearn for the security of "Knowing" what will happen and how things will turn out. For the most part, the gift of prophecy is the part of us that simply "goes by faith".

When you work with the unlimited universal level of consciousness, the desperate urge to "Know the Future" diminishes and it is replaced with a faith that you will know, what you need to know, when you need to know it. This, of course, is only true if you keep the channels of communication open. In point of fact this will relieve you of many of life's worries and concerns and leaves you free to enjoy and savour the wonderful present.

Today this gift is known as:
Channelling   Trance   Precognition   Premonition
Hunch   De já vu   Gut instinct   Day-dreams
And also dreams, which given time, will actually come true.

A lady in Wellington told me the following story on a radio talk back show. She awoke one morning having dreamt that her family had been driving in the car, on the motorway into Wellington for an outing. Then the car burst into flames and the family were all killed in the fire.

Weeks later she and her husband and children were driving into Wellington, when she was overcome with the most intense feeling of doom. She yelled at her husband, "Stop the car, Stop the car", and luckily, he did as she requested. "Get out Get Out" she screamed at them all, as she pulled the children from the car and ran down the road screaming "Come away Come Away".

Within minutes the car exploded, and was completely incinerated in the flames. Her prophetic dream was a message that saved all of their lives.

When you are using this form of communication you will use the expression "I know" a great deal. It has commonly been called the gift of faith and trust, for it will inspire you to act without any substantive evidence that you are correctly assessing a situation correctly. Somehow you will "just know" that you will,

Get the job
Be in the right place at the right time
Know the right car to buy
Be the best person to hire
Take the best course of action
You will get the money that you need
Be okay and that everything will work out absolutely fine

Have you ever been speaking to someone, and out of your mouth came the most amazing piece of wisdom, insight or perspective. In fact you were quite shocked and surprised at how "wise" you were. That is channelling. It is the ability for you to stand aside from your body, or be overshadowed, and allow an angel to use your voice to speak to someone.

My first clear experience of channelling was at a workshop I was presenting. The participants were discussing a concept, and I was walking around the room listening to snippets of conversation from each group. Something caught my attention and I overheard someone say that "they were a victim" in a particular set of circumstances. Suddenly, I was galvanised into action and strode purposefully back to the front of the room.

With a strong clear assertive tone of voice I spoke at length about the need for personal responsibility. The spiritual reality is that everyone and everything that happens to us, is of own making and we have drawn it/them into our lives so that we can grow and learn from the situation.

At the conclusion of my "little speech" I went to sit down. As I was lowering myself into the chair, I was dropped from a height of 15 – 20 centimetres to land on the chair with a great bump. I gasped with surprise and uttered "Who was that?" and I heard "It was me, Michael". Then I knew that Archangel Michael had been channelling through me, and it was his clear-cut assertive energy that had expressed his wisdom to the class.

People have channelled the high souls of the universe to, write books, compose music and to deliver sermons, speeches or blessings.

At one spiritualist church service I attended, the guest medium for the day was a gentleman. His eulogy for the service was a channelled message and this was the first time I had ever seen a person go into trance to deliver a sermon.

I have witnessed many people being overshadowed by master beings, but never someone in full trance in this manner. The man never blinked, never moved his eyes, and his hands remained in the same prayer like position for the duration of his message. Sadly, the beings speaking through him were not of the highest order as his message was lacking in inspiration, love, and light, and most of us fell asleep as though all the energy was being drained from us.

Going into trance is a natural gift of the perception of prophecy. When people are using the gift of prophecy they often sleep walk, sleep talk, or drive the car from A to B, and not know how they got there. As children and adults they often drift "away with the fairies" into a fantasy world if they are bored or alone.

I actually do not believe we need to learn to go "into trance", but rather to discipline ourselves to stay out of it. That is; we need to live in the present moment, and not drift away somewhere and miss the opportunity to "Seize the day". We need to be 100% in our bodies, until it is appropriate to trance out and channel your angels.

You may, like me, have experienced a situation where people who are excessively affected by drugs or alcohol, behave as if they are someone different or behave very differently. I know that at these times they are not 100% in control of their bodies. So trying to reason with them is out of the question, because I do not really know whom I am dealing with. I have often wondered if this is why some people say, after a "big night out", that they cannot remember anything. Maybe they were astro tripping or gone somewhere and a confused soul took the opportunity to "pop in" for a drink.

There are varying degrees of trance defined as follows:
Meditation   Deep Meditation   Semi Trance   Full Trance

Many spiritual healers do trance healing work. They assist earthbound souls remember their big picture, and return home to the universe to regain their spiritual direction. This form of channelling has been called:
Trance healing   Rescue work   Boogie busting   Ghost busting   Entity releasing and Soul clearing.

Many people have unfolded their channelling ability to allow master souls, beings of the highest order, and Archangels to deliver messages of wisdom, knowledge, truths and love.

They do this so that others may hear the age-old truths and feel the enormous joy and sense of oneness that fills the universe.

My First encounter of a woman who channelled Master Beings was an experience I shall never forget. She was the communicator for a group of Masters that collectively called themselves the "I Am Consciousness. From the first word this team of beings spoke, my heart was suffused with a love and acceptance that I have never encountered from a human being. I "knew" I was reconnecting with the Great I Am, God or The Creator. It was an instant recognition that I was indeed an expression of, and a part of the godhead. I felt with absolute clarity, that my true nature as a soul was the love that connects every living thing in the universe.

Your angels may have also used other people's mouths to channel messages to you so that they can, encourage you, counsel you, inspire you and expand your horizons. The universe is always talking to you softly, and if you are not listening, they will use anyone or anything to catch your attention when they need to.

Because your gift of prophecy is always scanning ahead it will lead you to have many de já vu experiences. This is that canny or weird sensation that "I've been here before." It can be a conversation, a group of people, a house, a town or knowing where to find a place or building in a city that you have never been to before, and yet you know you have.

This experience of de já vu comes about through your dreamtime. When you go to sleep you astro travel into the future and have experiences there. You may visit cities, have job interviews, enter houses and dwellings or visit people and have conversations with them. Upon waking up in the morning you will know that you have had dreams, but will be unable to recall the overview or details. Days, weeks, months or years later you will enter a situation and be flooded with that weird sensation that is described as "I've been here before".

When you dream of an event in the future that comes to pass, it is described as a prophetic dream. If you receive information about or perceive a future event, in your waking state, this is called a premonition. You see the gift of prophecy is always scanning ahead and therefore is only ever senses the future. Since these precognitions are often of an impending disaster, the people who make these predictions are often called "Doomsday Prophets".

Through out history people have had dreams or precognitions of the future such as; famines, floods, airline crashes, ships sinking, wars and natural disasters. They have also foreseen the deaths or assassinations of famous people like Princess Diana, Martin Luther King, President Kennedy, Ghandi, Arch Duke Ferdinand and Lord Louis Mount Batten. Of course they do have the ability to pick up on happy events and outcomes equally as easily.

In 1992 I inspired and organised a group of 17 people to take a two-week trip to Hawaii with me. Six weeks before we were due to leave, my employment contract was terminated. This left me unemployed with no future job in sight, so I was unable to go. I was very disappointed because it was also to be a family holiday as my mum was going, and also my sister and her husband. It would have been the first time we all went away on holiday together since I was 23yrs old.
Anyway, it was arranged that I would meet them at the airport upon their return, and bring them back to my home for a welcoming home dinner and to hear all the news.
As Mum walked out into the arrivals hall and came into view, I immediately sensed that something was different about her. She looked wonderfully tanned and was very happy and excited, however I sensed something was wrong.

That night as I went to bed I "Knew" that she was going to pass on in the near future. It was as if her inner light or fire was dimming and I knew she would pass over within 2-3 years. It actually turned out to be 3 years and 8 months, when her ailing heart finally wore out. Knowing she would be leaving us, I made a point of telling her through many letters, cards and phone calls, what an amazing influence she had been in my life. I miss her physical companionship dearly and yet feel at peace that all was well between us before she passed on. I am looking forward to seeing her and catching up on the news as we always did, after I pass on.

Prophetic types love their beds and sleeping, as this allows them the spiritual freedom to go wherever in the universe they choose, and experience what ever they want to. When they feel spirit needing to communicate with them they will take a very small nap, and wakeup refreshed and ready to continue their day. They are very sociable creatures, good communicators, and make very good executives and managers of people.

They are naturally drawn to the theatrical, fantasy and whimsical side of life, for they know innately that life is just a game to be enjoyed. When you are operating out of the gift of prophecy your aura will have a great deal of purple in it, and you may even be drawn to wear the colour purple. This gift will stimulate your curiosity about magic, miracles, psychic matters, the paranormal, science fiction and the spiritual, mystical, magical side of life.

Being in touch, first hand as it were, with the universe, they usually have a lucky or prosperous streak running through their lives. This sensitivity to the unending supply of all things spiritual and temporal will draw them to be in the right place at the right time, to collect or enjoy life's goodies. They love to be spontaneous and pleasure seeking, which draws them naturally to the luxurious things in life.

In 1980 my angels used a gentlemen at one of my workshops to ask me if I had any audiocassette tapes that he could buy to listen to at home. I laughed nervously and said "Oh no! I only do workshops and consultations". In 1981 the same situation was repeated in another city, and it happened again in 1982. Each time my response was the same "I only do workshops and consultations, not tapes."
It was 1997 and 15 years later when in I woke up one morning and said to myself, "today I have to make tapes." It took 3 phone calls, 1 failed attempt at recording and only 4 weeks in total, until I had 4 tapes sunk and ready for sale.
Little did I know that all those years ago, those sensitive gentlemen were channelling my angels so that they could bring a new idea into my conscious mind. It was seemingly preposterous idea at the time, and yet the idea only took 15 years to come to fruition.

The larger the new project is, the longer lead time they give us to get adjusted to the growth step, confidence level, and awareness it will take to achieve it. Maybe your angels have given you 3-4 hints, in advance, about a situation. Sometimes it's a hint to change, hold back, or not doing something, on the other hand they could be hinting for you to stop procrastinating and get on with it. Because your gift of prophecy knows how things will turn out, you will often procrastinate before moving into action and actually doing the activity required.

The gift of prophecy is the fun part of us – the spontaneous, curious, social part of us all. The facet in each of us that loves good stories, food, drama, theatre, wine and above all a remembrance that life is for living and enjoying. Your psychic sense of smell and taste is associated with this perception, so you "smell" the perfume of departed loved ones or angels. Perhaps you have smelt something burning and then one hour later you burn the toast or dinner.

This gift constantly stimulates us to want to know the big picture of our own lives and it reminds us that we are but visitors here and the Universe, the All, or the Cosmos is truly our home and where we belong.

**Be still and listen,
for your Angels speak softly**

Clairvoyance

The second language is that of Clairvoyance, which is a French word that means clear seeing. This is the most historically well-known form of spiritual communication, and is recognised through every tribe, culture, race, religion, philosophy and civilisation in the world. People who had visions and dreams were considered sacred or holy, and selected by spirit as special vessels and preceptors of the desires of the Gods. Often these special mediums would go into drug induced trances or meditation to gain insights from the Gods. This was particularly true if they were seeking answers about the welfare, direction, or wisest decision to implement over matters that would affect the whole nation, tribe or group.

This perception has to do with your ability to receive pictures or images from the your angels in your minds eye or third eye. You will get these images through one of the following methods:

Visions	Dreams	Symbolic
Dreams		
Visualisation	Imagination	Symbols
Seeing into people	Seeing an aura	
Along with a Photographic memory		

One very famous dreamer and dream interpreter was "Joseph" of biblical fame. Moses had a vision of the burning bush, and Archangel Gabriel visited Mary to tell her she had been chosen to carry the Son of God. Leonardo de Vinci had visions of helicopters, bicycles, and other twentieth century inventions. People with visual connections to spirit like this, were often persecuted as witches, devil worshippers, or as having the evil eye.

Thanks to the Spiritualist movement in Victorian times, the gift of clairvoyance became safe and even fashionable. Today it is considered a very desirable talent, and people with clairvoyant talents are much sought after, because of their ability to sense the future. Being a clairvoyant is one of the new spiritual professions. Just as you might seek medical advice from a doctor, you would seek spiritual insight from a psychic.

If you are communicating with your angels through this perception of clairvoyance, you will dream in colour, as not all dreams are coloured ones. They will be like a movie or stream of consciousness that is unfolding inside your mind. Furthermore, your dreams will often be symbolic which means you will need to interpret the insights that they hold. Each dream will hold clues, answers and insights into an experience you are having, or a pattern in your life, or the solution to a problem.

Added to this, is the fact that as individual souls, we are all at different levels of awareness so the same symbol can mean different things to each of us. This is why books on dream interpretation can be very confusing and misleading. There are however a small list of universal symbols that apply to us all. They are as follows:

Horse	The symbol of knowledge
Water	The Holy Spirit, The All, The Oneness, The vastness of Spirit
Dog	Devotion
Flying	Freedom, or escaping from life
Car	Your direction. Who was driving it, you or someone else?
Falling	Fear of failure

Teeth	Your wisdom
Birth	A new idea or state of consciousness
Death	Change of a state of consciousness
Snake	Healing abilities, Healing or revenge
Train	On track or in a rut
Ship or Boat	How you are moving through life. Is it a yacht, rowboat, or a battle ship
House	Your state or level of consciousness
Being Naked	in a public place is showing your true self to people

Strangely, nightmares only seem to occur through the gift of clairvoyance, as we "see" awful scenes, happenings or things in our dream state. When you astro travel to a past life you will be able to "see" the scene, much like a movie playing in your mind. Otherwise you will be high above a scene and you will view it in a very detached way, much like having a bird's eye view of the situation.

I have stepped into time warps when visiting Rome, Venice, London, and Paris and seen small time segments from the past as if I were back in time living it. The horses, costumes/clothes, heraldic banners, smells and the pageantry and opulence were so real it was as if I were really there. Minutes, and a few paces later, I was back in the hustle and bustle of the twentieth century.

When your angels are using this language to give you hints on your Direction, choices, or options, they will use things to attract your visual attention like:

Movies programmes	Television
Books	Imagination
Magazine headlines	Travel agents posters
Adverts in newspapers	Posters

At the age of four, I "saw" my first angels in the form of coloured balls of light that floated around the ceiling in my

room. At the age of ten, while I was lying on a grassy hilltop at the back of the farm cloud watching, I saw two hands in the sky. One hand was reaching upwards and the other extended downwards as if they were trying to reach each other.
When I was a teenager my current beau asked me to go with him to see the movie "The Agony and the Ecstasy" starring Charlton Heston. It was Hollywood's version of the life of Michael Angelo. I shrieked and wept when I saw for the first time, the centre- piece of the ceiling of the Sistine chapel. For there, up on the huge screen, for the entire world to see, were the hands from my vision in the clouds.

Clairvoyance, like prophecy, has been very sensationalised. Many people I meet don't believe they are clairvoyant because they can't foretell people's future. Nor do they receive grand and detailed visions like other people do when meditating. Please don't compare yourself to other people, because you, like me, will always find people who have experiences different to, or beyond our realm. Having said this, rest assured that your personal gift of "inner seeing" works perfectly.

It shows up as:
Seeing the perfect chair or picture to finish the decoration of the room.
Seeing beauty in nature, the sea- the sky.
Being able to plan our projects in your minds eye.
Being organised and orderly.
Seeing past lives in people's auras.
Seeing the mirror of the soul in people's eyes.
Seeing (often in slow motion) a way of fixing something
for example; a chair, a door, or a garment.
Imagining, or envisaging how a house or room can look or be decorated.
Visualising the way you want the grounds around your home landscaped.
Being artistic either through art or music.

Fashion designing.
Writing or recording notes as a student and then being able to recall what you have written. (Photographic mind)
Compartmentalising or breaking a project down into boxes or segments or manageable pieces, while still being able to retain the overview or big picture.
Seeing nature spirits, divas and fairies.
Having an imaginary playmate.
It is the spiritual language of visions, symbols and signs.

My workshop participants have often asked me if their visual messages are only their imagination? My reply is "what is imagination?" The dictionary defines it as:
"A mental faculty forming images or concepts of external objects not present to the senses"
I personally feel this is a perfect description of how clairvoyance works.

Always endeavour not to get caught up in trying to prove you had an experience, or that you perceived what you did. Many of my night class students seek my validation as to whether they "really saw" what they did. I often answer their request in the following manner.
> Can you prove to me that angels exist? You can't.
> Can you prove to me that you had a dream last night? You can't.
> Can you prove to me that feeling of love that you have for someone? You can't.

Even though we can't prove these things to one another, we accept that they are real because we all have these experiences in common. Have faith in yourself and always trust your own perceptions and intuition.

When I was living in London I went through a stage of seeing the face of a dear friend (who lived in Australia), everywhere I looked. I "Saw" her on the tube, on the bus, at the supermarket, it seemed as if she was haunting me because I saw look-alikes of her everywhere. Finally I rang her, and her response was "Thank goodness you have rung at last. I have been sending you messages to call me as I have lost your phone number. I have really been having troubles and I did so much want to talk them over with you, and find a solution".

This spiritual gift has a real affinity with nature. Many cultures receive animal and nature symbols as messages from God and the Universe.
Over the years I have seen angels, as the typical winged kind, appear to me personally
    Above hospitals, prisons, mental health centres
    Above countries they oversee
    Around other people
    Helping people pass on or over

Your gift of clairvoyance will have these types of experiences easily as long as you attune your self to the highest energy possible. Maybe through this gift you have seen a soul who has passed on or what you might call a ghost or an entity.

My future mother in law passed on 6 weeks before I married her son. At her funeral I saw her standing beside the coffin, as large and as happy as life itself. It was a strange experience as everyone about me was mourning, and I felt so happy for her. My happiness was because she had been suffering with malignant cancer, and now she was free from the trauma associated with such an illness.

It is a very fascinating experience when a persons past life overshadows their current persona, and you can "see" what they were, and the time that they lived. From this you can often see the strengths and habits that emerge today from that past experience.

When I was only eleven I remember seeing my mother dressed to go to a ball. She was lit up like a Christmas tree, a fairy godmother, a luminous beautiful woman. The memory of it is as clear today, all these years later, as it was the night it happened. I was in my twenties when I was to find out that she conceived her last child that night. What I had seen was all the white light being poured into her aura by my baby brother and his team of Angels, in preparation for his conception.

I love to show people how to see auras, as it is very exciting when you recognise it for the first time. Children see them so naturally and will often draw a picture of you totally in the colour purple or red.

It is your aura and energy field that they see and draw. If you do not understand this you might say things such as "Mummy is not purple", or "That's not how I look, I am not red". So begins the process of shutting down their natural spiritual gifts and their third eye. Think about it from their point of view for a moment, if their all knowing Mummy or daddy can't see it, then it can't be real.

The gift of clairvoyance is the natural administrator in us all. The person who has this gift loves things to be visually pleasing, and often sees the beauty in nature missed by others. Their homes are usually aesthetically pleasing, and the colour schemes will harmonise to bring about a sense of peace and calm.

When you are using this gift your body temperature will change and you will have cold hands and feet, even on a warm day. These visionary types get distracted very easily as things will catch their eye. It is this habit that gives them the tendency to be late, for everything. A natural desire to always feel peaceful and calm will make it easy for these types to meditate.

The love of nature will make these people very concerned about our environment, and they also feel a great affinity with all of god's creatures, an the land and in the sea. To "see" fairies, elves, pixies and nature spirits within trees and forests is a natural longing of the soul for clairvoyants. These romantic types are often away in a magical, fantasy, perfect world of their own creation. When you are using this gift your aura will be suffused with a golden yellow glow.

Clairaudience

This psychic gift is the method by which your angels "literally" talk to you. It is actually the gift of mental telepathy. They think the thoughts and you receive them in your mind. This form of communication is called clairaudience, which the dictionary defines as;
The supposed facility of perceiving, as if by hearing, that which is inaudible.
This is the reason that people find it so difficult to discern whether they are "hearing" their own thoughts, or those being sent by angels.

I often use the term "My angels told me" when I am having a conversation with my sister. On many an occasion, she has asked "Why must that be your angels thoughts, don't you have good ideas yourself?" It is not easy to describe how you know the subtle difference between your own thoughts and those of your angels to a sceptical person.

With the exception of an extreme emergency, your angel's voices or thoughts are soft in vibration. They feel like a cool breeze as they wander through your mind. They have a sense of illumination, inspiration, even a hint of mirth, and are like chocolates for the soul. If you have endless uncontrollable babble or mind talk going on in your head, it is not your angels. That endless chatter that sounds like a family of monkeys is the collective consciousness and spiritual pollution that permeates the air-waves.

Many years ago I read a story about a spiritual master who was in the presence of a group of demanding, self centred people. They were bombarding him with endless questions and senseless statements regarding his beliefs and values. Finally he had had enough and shouted, "Please stop walking through my mind with your muddy boots on", after which, silence reigned.

Clairaudience is a French word that means Clair = clear and hearing = audience, so clairaudience translates into clear hearing. For this reason you will need, and look forward to silence, if this is your primary mode of spiritual communication. You need the quiet time to be able to hear yourself think, and to receive thoughts and messages from your angels.

Your angels may wake you up between 2am and 4am in order to "talk" to you, as the collective consciousness is quieter at this time and you can hear them more clearly. On these occasions they may just want you to listen to what they are saying, or they may want to flood your mind with a bigger message so you will need to get a pad and pen and do inspired writing.

Over centuries, right up to the present time many people have been ridiculed, persecuted or institutionalised for hearing voices. One of the most famous cases of someone "hearing God" talking to them was featured in the late 1990's by the two films which were made about Joan of Arc. Her personal conviction that the messages were to be acted upon changed the fate of a nation, and ultimately led to her being burnt at the stake.

I too, along with many of my clients, have received specific spoken direction, and the reason for it, from a force much higher than my team of angels, which I still think of as God.

A week after I was discharged from hospital, I was quietly sitting at the dining room table in my sister's home, having a cup of coffee. Then, like a bolt from the blue this strong

masculine voice said, "Julia we need you to write another book". I got such a shock I spun around expecting to find a person standing behind me.
When I recovered my senses I asked, "What about? What do you want me to write about?"
"Your experiences, so that people will recognize that they have had the same experiences, and therefore they may come to accept their own spiritual nature. We need them to be more open and trusting of their own truths, intuitions and to appreciate their team of angels. Could you do this for us?"
It was in the month of June 2000 when, with great reservation, I agreed to accept their mission. However I was very concerned about publishing, printing and distribution as this was very new territory for me.
The heavenly response to my concerns was that it did not matter how many books were sold as becoming an international author was not the reason for doing to work. Rather, they said, it was to record, for posterity "My own spiritual truth" in order that it would help confirm the truth in others. My life purpose was not about being internationally acclaimed and the fame and fortune that ensued from it, but rather in sharing a spiritual message.
This insight sat very comfortably within me, so I was able to go about the task with courage and enthusiasm.

Many children hear spiritual voices and are not old enough to discern between angels and earthbound souls. The voices they hear that want them to do mischievous things, are not their angels, but confused souls who want them to play with them. The end result is that the child ends up in trouble with their parents, teachers at school, or even their friends, yet the confused souls have had a good time.

If a child has this gift along with clairvoyance, they will see and hear souls who have passed on. Perhaps you saw the movie "The Sixth Sense" which illustrated this ability so clearly. If these gifted children have parents who

don't understand these abilities, the child will be very much misunderstood, and even maligned.
Clairaudient children will also have a natural flair for leadership and a tendency to be stubborn and wilful.

"Angel talk" always brings out the best in everyone, encouraging, and confirming the spiritually right and appropriate thing to do.
Clairaudience is known by the following characteristics;
1   Hearing what is really being said
2   Discernment of energy. i.e. whose thought/feeling is this?
3   Awaking with repetitive thoughts ideas or solutions
4   Counselling or listening skills
5   A wonderful memory for the sounds of voices
6   A natural flair or ear for language
7   Mental telepathy
8   Hearing the truth behind words

Mental telepathy is the language of thoughts and sounds, which is mainly heard inside your head, however at times it can be outside your head, as if another human being has spoken to you.
For example have you ever,
Heard your name called and there's no one there?
Heard the phone ringing before it rang?
Thought something, and someone else said it, or vice versa?
Thought of someone and they rang you?
Thought of someone and you see them the next day or week?
Been able to gauge a persons intentions or motives very accurately?
Heard souls who have passed on "talking"?

As a child, my brothers and sisters and I would go up into the bush at the back of the farm and play for hours.

Often I heard voices talking and I remember wondering at the time, how far away are those people that their voices can carry on the wind like this. I used to hear voices speaking in Maori, which I could not understand, but I certainly recognized the language.

Because of the wonderful training I received over the years, I have had the privilege of hearing many souls speak to me, especially in my past life clearing work. However one experience that will stay forever in my heart, was the conversations I had with Chief Dan George over the five weeks I spent in Canada in 1998.

The first time I heard the rich timbre of his voice I recognized the sound instantly, as I had known this voice all my life. I could not put a name to it, but I knew this glorious wise voice. He welcomed me home, and told me the ancient ones were glad that I had returned home. While I enjoyed my vacation in Ottawa, Quebec, Montreal, Winnipeg, Calgary and Vancouver, this wise old man and I had brief talks each day. Each time we communicated I was touched in the heart by his quiet deep love and acceptance of me.
It was not until I reached Torfino on Vancouver Island, that I was to discover the identity of my Indian Elder. There, in the Eagle Aerie Art Gallery, while I was admiring the work of Roy Henry Vickers, I heard that divine voice again. It was coming from a video being played on the television set and it was reciting poetry to the images of Roy Henry Vickers paintings. I sat, tears streaming down my face, as I heard my old friend's voice, this time in a room for all to hear.
I rushed up to the receptionist and asked who the voice was. "It is the artist, Roy Henry Vickers" she replied. "Has he passed on? I blurted. "No" she said. I told her I had been hearing that voice in my head for 5 weeks now. Who is it?" I babbled. "Oh " she said, "That is Roy channelling Chief Dan George". I heaved a great sob, and was too overcome to speak. Chief Dan George had been an actor in many of the films I had seen as a child. No

wonder I knew his wonderful voice and dry sense of humour. I haven't heard from him since I made a commitment to him to return to Canada and do my spiritual work, when the timing was right. I look forward to the day when we will speak again, as my heart misses him very deeply.
The last movie I can recall seeing him in was "Little Big Man" where he starred along side Dustan Hoffman. He passed on in the latter part of the 1990's.

With the gift of clairaudience you are able to sense what people are saying, even though you do not speak their language. When you are reading a letter you will hear the words in your head as if the person is speaking to you. Perhaps, like me, you have read a biography about someone you know, and you can hear his or her voice as you read the book. This was particularly true for me when I read Michael Caine's book, because I could hear his voice, with its east end accent, in every page.

Perhaps you have discovered that you are a very good judge of character, because this is also a characteristic of the gift of clairaudience. It is the ability to hear behind what people are really saying to the intention behind the words. In essence, you will hear the inner truth in a person's statements. Also, let me say this, the **Truth**, no matter how bad it is, is paramount to a person who has clairaudience as their first perception.

This perception thinks in terms of What, When, Where, Why and Who. It is this unbiased, factual, no nonsense approach to life that makes people natural born leaders. If this is your primary source of communication with the universe, then you will have a very active enquiring mind. Your quest for the answers to "What is really going on or happening here" is rather like having the mind of a policeman. Or you may have a psychologists' curiosity about "Why does a person or people behave in that way". These two inquiring approaches to situations will be a driving force in your life.

Your inquisitive mind will arouse your natural curiosity about people, behaviour patterns, cultures, customs and ways of life.

Your Angels will send you thoughts about how to solve problems, implement new ideas and or about how you can be of better service to people. They will also assist you with money matters, relationships and direction. You will receive the information as good or bright ideas that come as if a bolt from the blue.

They will always tell you what is for your highest good, so if you want a biased or particular outcome or answer, don't ask your angels. For they love you enough to honour that which is for your highest good, even if it isn't what you want to hear. My angels often talk to me in humorous terms, helping me to see the funny or cheerful side of situations. If you dare to walk on the light hearted side of life and you will always be in the company of angels.

While walking down the main street of Bundaberg, Australia, I saw a 4year old boy walking towards me dressed like a cowboy. He looked terrific and had his six guns drawn shooting anyone in sight, acting as if he was the sheriff keeping law and order for all the folks in his town'. As he approached me he pointed his gun and made a sound as if he had fired at me.
I clutched my chest and made the appropriate grunts and staggered as if I had been shot, playing along with his little fantasy. He looked so shocked, and reacted as if he had really shot me. Then he grinned from ear to ear because someone had acknowledged him. His Mum smiled and gave me a look of gratitude, that I would actually enter his world for a few seconds and play his game. It was such a small gesture but it made my day to "play as children" even if for only a brief moment, and a smile was firmly planted on my face for the rest of the day.

Mental telepathy is a very potent gift, because what you think about most of the time usually comes to pass. Thoughts are things, therefore very real and powerful forces. This is the basis upon which spells, voodoo, boning, and superstition are formed. If you believe something will be, so it will be. For example, if you keep saying you are unlucky in love that is exactly what will keep happening. If you fill your mind with thoughts of financial lack, those thoughts will continue to create financial lack in your life. The universe will rearrange itself to suit the thought patterns that you are transmitting.

For this reason it is important to discern whose thoughts you are having, what is your truth, and what is your true reality. Do you allow your mind be filled with the collective consciousness's negative, restrictive view and babble or do you tap into the fifth dimension and the higher spiritual realms? The choice is yours.

I was sitting on a seat in a pedestrian mall reading a newspaper when a lady walked by and it was obvious she was a person who lived on the street. Her appearance marked her circumstances, and her worldly possessions packed in carrier bags were weighing her arms down. As she passed in front of me I heard three distinctly different voices arguing in her head. Never before had I heard the souls around a person that clearly. It was as if all three were standing directly in front of me. I was flooded with compassion for the woman as it must have been nigh impossible for her to discern the difference between her own thoughts and the arguing trio. No wonder her life was in the situation it was.

People with this gift as their first perception have a huge love for mankind and humanitarian issues. Natural leadership is their strength, and encouraging people to be self- empowered, independent and capable, is their great love.

The natural sense of justice and fairness within this perception will make them comfortable mixing with all levels of society.

They have very little regard for pomp, status, prestige and social froth.

To this end, they are never afraid to approach the person at the very top of an organisation or to meet people from any walk of life. They will be unconventional in their approach to life, and if told something can't be done, will set out to prove the teller wrong. Murder mysteries and psychological thrillers appeal to their sense of problem solving and understanding of the human psyche.

A childlike natural curiosity about how things work will dominate their lives, as they seek to know more about things, people and life. Once their mind has mastered a task, or skill, they will get tired and bored with it. Why? Because they love a challenge, and the thrill of learning something new.

At the communication level in your aura, clairaudience shows up as the colour red. If you are strong in this gift you may even love to wear red and count it as your favourite colour.

Clairaudient people are most often very careful in their choice of words for they know their lives will be effected by everything they think and say. When you recognise this gift within yourself you will appreciate the immense power in sounds, statements and words. When you attune this gift to the highest realms, it will allow you to hear the heavenly choirs, the rustle of Angel's wings, and universal harmonics. You will recognise the immense healing power and energy behind sounds.

Clairsentience (Feeling or Healing)

The last of the four languages that your angels will use is Clairsentience. This is the spiritual language of feelings and it is often called the gift of healing. It is the language based on energy, vibrations and attunement to the feelings of people, houses, restaurants, shops and countries.

Have you ever lived in a house or flat because it felt good or conversely had to move out because the energy was so bad? Over the years I have heard stories of people who have not taken flights, ferry trips, and car journeys because it "did not feel right" to do so. Not a very logical reaction, but oh so accurate, as those people saved themselves from disasters, some of which would have fatal.

This perception has often been described as following your heart, instincts or feelings, and it is the most acutely sensitive facet of all the four perceptions. Strong feeling impressions through this gift are very difficult to forget or shake off.

My strongest feeling experience took place in Sydney, Australia. A friend had asked me out to dinner at a hotel in Kings Cross. We duly arrived, were seated, and the drink waiter came to our attendance almost immediately. Neither of us wanted an aperitif, so we opted to choose our meal and then select a bottle of wine to compliment it. While we sat talking and waiting for our food waiter to take our order, I began to feel very uncomfortable, and the feelings escalated into horrendous pains in the stomach.
We continued to talk and still the waiter never appeared to take our dinner order. After half an hour I could stand it no

longer, and finally said how ill I felt and that I wanted to go home. My date heaved a huge sigh of relief and said "I am glad you spoke up, because I feel awful as well". We both stood up and took our leave, causing no inconvenience to anyone, as we had not had the chance to order anything. It was not until the next day that it became apparent why our angels had intervened and prevented us from ordering. They clearly wanted us both pout of the environment of the restaurant and hotel.

Meanwhile, we both felt so physically upset that eating a meal elsewhere was out of the question. We walked, window shopped and talked, ending up having a light snack three hours later.

The next day the newspaper headlines heralded the news of a fatal stabbing that took place in the very hotel where we were going to dine. How did the person die? From fatal wounds to the stomach. Although the event happened at 2.30am, long after we had left, our sensitivity was telling us that a very negative incident was already in the making.

The spoken word of this gift is "I feel". I feel good about this, I don't feel good about that, I feel I should act today, I feel that this is right. This feeling sensitivity is more commonly accepted as being woman's intuition, because women are generally the more feeling of our two sexes.

Over the years I have met people who have opened there homes to me and leant me their cars, after a single and brief meeting.

An employer in London entrusted me with their considerable wealth and a key to the safe, after I had been working for them for only two weeks. They left me in charge of their home for eight weeks, without ever having someone come to the home and check up on me. All of this trust they bestowed on me was only based on feelings. I knew they had contacted ex-employers and checked my references, yet it still seemed an incredible act of trust to go on vacation, leaving a virtual stranger in care of their home and its possessions. This is the power of trusting your instincts or feelings.

With this gift your angels will touch your sensitivity, heart or gut with a strong feeling impression about a situation, person, direction, or solution to a situation.

If clairsentience is your strongest perception your dreams, will tend to be visually vague, but you will awake with a very strong residual feeling that may last for hours or even days. This strong residual feeling is the important message or clue from the dream and you will have to decipher its relevance to your daily affairs. The gift of feeling or healing is also characterized by,
- Being able to heal with a touch.
- Attunement or sensitivity to animals.
- Very capable or manually dexterous hands.
- Automatic or creative writing.
- Sensing things by touch, ie. psychometry.
- Choosing clothes by how the fabric feels to you.
- Selecting fruit and vegetables by touch or squeeze.
- Having a dream that the feelings were so strong they last 1-3 days.
- Feeling or picking up someone else's back pain or headache
- Having a green thumb

Healing people is another integral part of this perception and if this is your primary mode of angelic connection you will be a natural healer. Whether this takes the form of, Medicine, Nursing, in a hospital or within the Community. You may feel a need to take training in a modality like,
- Massage therapy in all its forms
- Chiropractic or Physiotherapy
- Reiki, Spiritual healing or forms of energy work
- Reflexology
- Bowen technique
- Indian head massage, to name but a few.

These practices will allow energy to pour through your hands into the patient or client effecting a healing, which will take place on a physical, mental, spiritual, or emotional level.

Feeling, healing types of people also have a great affinity with animals, and will always opt to care for the lost cat, sick bird, or stray animal. They get very upset at the death of or the wounding of an animal. I know many sensitive souls that prefer animals to people, because they find human beings so very cruel and hurtful to one another.

When I was on a coach tour of Italy one of the couples received a phone call from their daughter to say that their three legged, blind, thirteen year old dog had been hit by a motorcar and severely damaged. The veterinary surgeon had quoted £700.00 for the surgery required to save its life. The daughter asked what they wanted to do, precede with surgery or let the dog pass on? So deep was their love for their beloved pet, they simply could not bear to part with their beloved companion so they chose to proceed with surgery. Even though they confessed that their financial situation was so stretched they could not afford dentures for the husband. This kind of sacrifice for the love of an animal is very typical of the feeling/healing type person.

Psychometry is the ability to sense and interpret the vibrations or energies of an inanimate object, such as a wallet or car keys.
This is a very common method is used by psychics to foretell things about a person during a psychic or spiritual reading. Everything is filled with energy, and objects in your personal possession will be filled with your aura or energy, therefore making it easy for a person to pick up and interpret things about you.
Everything you own has your energy in it, your house, car, clothes, jewellery, and even your tools of trade.

In one workshop I attended many years ago, we, the participants, worked together in pairs. The idea being that we had to give our partner a personal object of ours for them to read. The only item I had was my watch, which was just three days old. Since I had just purchased it three days prior to the seminar I thought that it would be "Too new" for me to have energized yet. How wrong I was, as I listened because the person proceeded to tell me things that they could not possibly have known.

Items that are second hand, such as clothes, and especially jewellery can retain the vibrations of their owner and this energy can influence you.

I was doing a reading for a person and I asked for an item that I could hold and do psychometry on. She took a ring off her finger and passed it to me, which I held, and preceded to share the things my sensitivity picked up from the item. Her face seemed blank the whole time, until I finally asked her "What is it? What is the matter?" She then told me that everything I had said was about her mum, and she was disappointed that I did not have a message for her. It was at this point I twigged and asked her "Whose ring is this?" "Its mine" was the reply "It was my mums but I have had it since she passed on". I then had to explain that her mum's energy was still in the ring and so it was not an object that truly represented her personally.

Your energy is the total collection of your thoughts, feelings and experiences, which makes your personal vibration very unique. People high in the gift of clairsentience need to develop their ability to discern and interpret what they are sensing. Otherwise they will take on the feelings of other people and think the feelings are their own. This is especially so of physical aches and pains.

For many years I spent money going to the doctor for illness's that were not mine. I displayed the symptoms, but the root cause was not there.

The gift of feeling is a wonderful sensory tool when you are travelling and do not speak the language of the country.

When I was in Hong Kong I met a young woman flight attendant at a bus stop, and we agreed to join up for companionship as we shopped at the Stanley Market. Ann and I had a wonderful time and as dinnertime approached we decided to eat some local fare for dinner. You know the idea; we wanted to eat where the locals ate, not at some fancy hotel restaurant. Kowloon was where we decided to look for a place to eat, and the only place that we found was at a crossroads junction in the night market. There, on the street corner, was a huge outdoor kitchen, fold up formica tables and chairs, and a throng of local people eating delicious smelling food.

Ann was so cautious and concerned about us getting food poisoning that she actually suggested we go home. At this juncture I heard my angels say, "Trust your feelings", so I told Ann what they had said. I suggested we both tune into the kitchen and the food and see what our feelings told us. It was unanimous, our feelings and sensitivity told us both it would be just fine to eat here. We had to visit the kitchen and point at our choices of food, because we had no idea how to order the food otherwise. We sat at the little portable table sharing a large bottle of chilled beer and the most scrumptious food out under the stars, amid the throng of workers and tourists alike. It was heavenly and the highlight of my trip to Hong Kong.

Your feeling gift is extremely sensitive to the vibrations of people. Non-more so than to souls who have passed on and are still earth bound.

When I was five, my English grandparents took our whole family on a Sunday outing to the Christchurch Museum. The rooms in the museum at that time were laid out in the style of the British Museum in London. My brother and I were particularly taken with the Egyptology room, filled with all its ancient artefacts. As I walked up to have a closer look at the open sarcophagus, I felt the mummy lying within it move. I got such a fright I screamed and ran terrified from the room. I "KNEW" I had felt the mummy move, no matter how much my family was determined to make me believe otherwise.

When I was 6 years old I loved attending Sunday school, especially for the singing, so when I turned 6 and allowed, I joined the Church Choir. Now this was in town where it is reported that in the 1800's the Maoris killed the Minister in the church, then they drank his blood and then had eaten his eyeballs. As you can imagine, at the age of six this was quite a gruesome story. All went well until the third week. In I went as usual to the church vestry where I donned my choir gown and then proceeded to the choir stalls in the church. I was looking around as I waited for the service to begin when I saw the silver chalice, in its box on the wall. This was the chalice from which had drunk the blood of the minister and as I stared at it I was filled with an overwhelming bad feeling. It was so intense that I could not sing and I fairly clawed my way out of my robes at the end of the service, and I never went back.
In both these cases, I had felt or sensed the presence of the souls who had passed on and yet were still earthbound.

It would take me well over thirty years to clarify, was the fact that, in sensing these souls at the tender ages of five and six, I was beginning my life's work. Is it any wonder that all these years later I am so heavily involved in past life healings, soul clearing and trance healing work?

You may have "felt" the presence of your angels as a feeling or vibration of;
Comfort   Never being alone
Great love   Immense peace
Healing   Great calm and acceptance
Everything is going to be alright

This is the language that "talks" to you in feelings, and its accuracy is often derided as being silly, emotional or stupid. Can you image men's reactions to my buying a car purely based on a good or great feeling about a vehicle. It simply does not seem what a rational mature person would do. However, it works for me, always has, and so why would I ever discontinue the practice.

You may experience,
    A feeling for a certain decision
    A feeling for a direction
    A feeling for the right time to act
    A feeling for the right place to be

People with this as their first perception, will be natural healers and are very huggable, cuddly individuals. Their enormous capacity to love people will fill their homes with such a welcoming atmosphere, that people will feel free to pop in at anytime. In fact, at times their home might feel like Grand Central station. They are very loyal to family members, jobs, and may retain the same friends for their entire life.

Feeling type people have a laid back approach to life, and will have a "Lets go with the flow" approach to life. They often have favourite and much loved, well-worn clothes, and prefers to be very casual and comfortable, bordering on sloppy in their dress style.

It is the gift of clairsentience within you that makes it hard for you to say or do things that would potentially hurt another person. You would much prefer to hurt yourself than another individual. Being loyal to yourself and putting yourself first does not come easy through this gift. In fact it would be extremely difficult and challenging. This gift loves the harmony of a happy team environment, whether this is within the family unit or at work.

The gift of Clairsentience has energy levels that are like an endless powerhouse, giving you the capacity to heal people, whether you are conscious of it or not. Blue is the aura colour that symbolises this gift and the gift of healing.

Your angels will use any one of the four languages to pass on their insights, answers, suggestions and direction. The more specific your requests for answers, help or guidance is, the easier it will be to recognize the answers when they come to you. By this process you will begin to realize your angels have been "talking" to you in the symbolic language of the soul for years and years.

**You are never without
the company of angels**

Protection and Connection

When you have a desire to connect with your Angels, spiritual guides and other ascended masters, you will be opening yourself up to the possibility of being connected to "All" the spiritual realms. Not all beings in the spiritual realms are of the purest light and highest intention. This distinction between the spiritual forces of "light and good" and "dark and evil" has been recognised for a very long time. So I am going to start this chapter off with the concept of **Protection.**

Throughout history, cultures, races, philosophies, and religions have used various forms of protection from forces that they considered evil, bad, malevolent, or malicious. As life and impending death were diminished or prolonged by famine, weather, and plague, so prayers, incantations and offerings were made to seek "Godly" protection and favour. Many cultures even used sacrifices of living things such as people or animals to appease the gods so they could attract the god's blessings for bountiful harvests and marriages, fair winds, good hunting, and safe travel.

Other forms of protection were Talismans worn around the neck, or amulets that were worn around the wrists and ankles. Animal and fish teeth, feathers, bear claws, stones, symbols, beads, and even garlic would be used to ward off what was considered evil spirits. The most widely used talismans in our modern Christian society are the cross, and a saint's medallion.

In the 21st century the need for spiritual protection is as relevant now as it ever was. In fact as the planet becomes more densely populated, the need to surround yourself with a positive and uplifting form of energy has become increasingly important. Mankind has always put a great deal of store and faith in the use of some form of protection that would connect them to a higher source of energy and keep them safe.

We may be more civilized by education, mass communication, transport, and technology, but spiritually we have the same need to protect ourselves as our forebears did. We need to protect ourselves from the thoughts and feelings of other people, the home, business and historical environments and from souls who have passed on.

Some of the forms of "energy altering" talismans that are in common use today are crystals, malachite carvings, carved whalebone, walrus tusks, beads, ying and yang symbols, prayer bracelets, and a variety of native American symbols. These were often hung on cord or leather, and worn around the neck. The wearers feel that the talismans enhance their well-being and lifted their spiritual vibration.

Over the centuries, because of reincarnation, we have left layers and layers of energy here; energy that is filled with our "human or limited views and emotions". This happens in the same way that you fill your home with your energy.
Some homes are filled with love, while others feel very strained and fraught with unhappiness or tension.

Logically this build up of thoughts and feelings is strongest in the countries that have been inhabited the longest. People's fears, anxieties, suppression, repression, and ways of survival are all in the "Spiritual Real Estate" and can be picked up, or tuned into, by anyone who is the slightest bit sensitive.

When you visit an old country you can feel the energy of its history quite palpably in many of the old buildings, market squares, churches and in the stately homes or castles. Some of the strongest experiences you can have of this nature are felt at historic, battle or religious sites.

When I toured Turkey we visited the Dardanelle's, and the battlegrounds and cemeteries that are there. The moment I got off the bus at Lone Pine Cemetery tears started to stream down my face, as I felt the huge wave of shock, loss and grief the hung in the air. So many youth gave their lives on this terrain for king and Country, and I could feel them as strongly as if they still had physical form. It was a very moving experience indeed.

Not only can you sense the residual emotions that are left behind, but you can also feel the presence of souls who are still earthbound. These earthbound souls have been called souls in karma, unclean spirits, evil spirits, ghosts, entities, and they are caught, stuck or trapped on and around Planet earth. In some way they got caught up in the "Game of life" and lost sight of their big picture, and the fact that they are an eternal being.

When you think about all the major events in history, such as wars, plague, famines, natural disasters, political and religious repression, conquests of countries and cultures, let alone family or tribal disputes, it is not surprising that many souls lost their way. Having said that let me say clearly that there is no such thing as a "lost" soul, because every soul knows exactly where it is. It may not be where it wants to be, and it may not know where to go, but it is definitely not lost, just stuck.

Somehow they got off track, so when they passed on they clung to the people or surroundings that they knew well. I know that if I thought that my current lifetime was all there was, I too, would probably cling to the things that were important to me when I passed on. I would want to stay connected to things like my loved ones or my material possessions.

A soul who is caught or earthbound is confused, fearful and or lacking in light, so it has a negative vibration. It is this negativity or darkness that you can feel in houses, places and around people, which frightens you if it catches you unawares. Have you ever walked into a room and been able to sense the vibrations in the atmosphere? Have you ever seen a dark form or shadow out of the corner of your eye? Similarly, have you ever been to a historic site and been able to feel presences in the environment?

On my honeymoon in 1969 we visited Larnoch Castle in Dunedin. We enjoyed roaming around the gardens, grounds and rooms, soaking up the history. There was a staircase leading from the 1st floor up into a turret, which had a magnificent view. Determined to make the most of our visit my husband started to ascend the stairs and I followed him. I reached the 5th stair and an incredible fear overwhelmed me. I was terrified, and froze on the spot, not being able to move my legs or cry out.
When I was able to force myself to move, I spun around and fled down all the staircases and out the front door into the garden. It took me over half and hour to regain my composure, and yet my husband had not felt anything at all. When we made enquiries about the house and it's history, we found out that it is reputed to be haunted. I had obviously felt the ghost's confused and negative energy.

If a soul gets caught up in the games of,
Control   Competition   Power   Glory
Devotion   Obligation   and Guilt,
They will remain earthbound until something happens and they can see the higher way. Healing souls in confusion has been going on for eons of time, in every culture in the world and it is recognised as,

* Exorcism
* Rescue Work
* Trance healing
* Cleansing evil spirits
* Dispossession
* Boogie busting

* Channelling
* White magic
* Healing work
* Ghost busting
* Light work
* Shattering Crystals

The basic precept to this form of healing work is that you would help a soul in confusion understand that it has passed on and therefore it no longer has a physical body.
Then you would need to ask the following questions,
- What is the last year that it remembers?
- What was the relationship between it and the person it is attached to?
- What emotions are keeping the two of them connected?

Then the next step is re-uniting them with their Angels, Guides, or Great Ancestors, depending on their beliefs. Finally, sending them off with their helpers to a school of learning and knowledge out in the universe so that they can regroup their experiences, and decide on a new spiritual direction.

An even simpler method of releasing souls in confusion that may be in your home is to fill your home with light, love, and angels. At this point, if you are comfortable, you can even say mentally or out loud in a firm but loving tone, "Why are you wasting your time around here? You know if you go with your Angels to the light, they will help you find the love, happiness, joy, acceptance, respect and fulfilment that you are really seeking".

Many cultures put a ban on a place where "bad" things like murders or suicides have happened, because they can sense the anguish, torment, or negative forces and energy are still present. After a time, this ban can be lifted by a special healing ceremony that is performed by a spiritual leader, priest or minister of religion. At this point the building or land is the pronounced spiritually safe and positive again.

There are schools of thought that call confused souls and the negativity that surrounds them, EVIL. Personally, I have never been able to subscribe to the concept of a person being evil, and never will. Why? Because at the heart of every soul is light, and if we are all a spark of divine energy or God, how can we be evil? Having said that I do accept that down through our history there are stories about people who have perpetrated some profoundly evil acts on their fellow man.

If you are doing any form of spiritual education or healing work as your part time or full time occupation then you need to be aware of how forces from the past may be trying to limit your progress.

I met a woman in one of my programs that had been a practicing clairvoyant for 22 years. She spoke to me about a book she had written on spiritual matters, and wanted to know why every time she went to take some form of pro-active action about getting it published, something would happen to sidetrack her. Her mum got ill, the dog was in a bad accident, her husband was made redundant, and they damaged the car in an accident. She was convinced by all these incidents that they were "signs" that she was not meant to publish her book, and she asked me for my thoughts were on the matter.

This was one of many stories I have heard over the years about a "force" trying to stop a spiritually aware leader from,
1. Becoming A Spiritual Healer or Therapist
2. Taking further professional development or training
3. Publishing a book that would bring more spiritual light to people

4. Speaking to groups or in front of a crowded room
5. Turning their spiritual talents into a professional business
6. Presenting workshops and classes
7. Doing an interview for a radio or newspaper

When your actions will bring more spiritual light or understanding to people, how could you possibly receive messages from your Angels or the universe, telling you not to proceed. Of course, they may suggest a better or more appropriate time for you too implement the idea. If you were a "Spiritual leader" or one in training, why on earth do you think your Angels would try to stop you doing something that would,
    a. Help you grow immensely
    b. Help other people grow or be healed
    c. Help the environment become more positive by your actions

The answer is, they wouldn't. If you have come to do conscious spiritual work this lifetime, then you are a light worker, and it is your angels role to work with you to co-create heaven on earth, not to hold you back. So then the question remains, who or what might be trying to hinder you progress? Are there dark or bad Angels influencing you, or your own deep memories about what happened to you when you did your spiritual work in the past?

In the first instance, it could be your memories about being persecuted for your beliefs and actions in a past life. You know that over the centuries they drowned, burnt, tortured, and crucified millions of us for our beliefs. This is an obvious answer and one you are probably well aware of. So let us take a closer look at what else it could it be.

There could be groups of souls who still feel that it is their mission to stop your progression, even though hundreds of years have gone by since you were all together. They can fit any of the following descriptions.

1. Religious orders trying to keep you in the monastery or convent.
2. Religious zealots who want you to keep the "One true faith".
3. Past life friends and loved ones who saw you killed for your beliefs are now trying to protect you from the same fate.
4. Souls who want to "use" you and your abilities for their Political and Financial gain, as they did in the past.
5. Souls who are jealous of your ability to influence and lead other people.
6. Souls who blame your leadership for their deaths and so their aim is to ensure that you never hold a leadership role again.

They feel that they have gained a great victory if they stop you taking that next steps forward towards ascension or mastery. This is why forms of protection and methods of connecting with Angels, Archangels and spiritual masters remains just as important at an advanced level, as it was when you began your conscious spiritual journey or quest.

When doing any spiritual work it is essential that you are protected or connected, and it is helpful to teach other people to do the same. For example you could say a simple prayer like,
- **I am open to receive**
- **I am light love and wisdom**
- **I am surrounded by angels and beings of the highest order**

Saying this prayer before meditation healings clairvoyance, channelling, group or class work sets the right energy for everyone to grow and learn in the best possible environment. At the end of your readings, meetings or sessions you can conclude with a closing prayer, or statement such as,
- **I am sealed with love**
- **I am love**
- **I am surrounded by light and I take it wherever I go.**

It makes a good spiritual discipline and practice to say a form of protection when you wake up in the morning because it will ensure that you do not get caught up in other people's grumpy moods. It is also great to do a connection process as you are going to sleep at night, because this will save you from having nightmares or bad astral trips and nightmares.

The Secret to enjoying a strong communication between you and your Angels, is to use a form of spiritual connection/protection daily, however it is most effective when it is done several times a day. This is most important when you are working with people, especially on a one to one basis. To keep your protection/connection routine simple you can think of it like a spiritual eating plan, or diet.

Upon waking =	spiritual breakfast
Mid morning =	spiritual coffee break
Lunch =	spiritual lunch
Afternoon Tea =	spiritual tea break
Dinner =	spiritual dinner time
Bed time =	spiritual suppertime.

Of course, like all good eating plans, it is always better for you to eat a little and often. Don't forget to change your form of protection or connection often. Like clothes, it gets boring wearing the same ones every day.

On occasions I have been called in to help people who are being physically punched, kicked, and overshadowed by a soul who wants to use their body. I had one woman writhing on the floor grunting as she "took" blows from the soul that was bothering her.

The soul was fighting to have her body all to itself. When I enquired as to when this all started, it seems that two years before she and a friend were trying to contact the spirit world, and this is was the outcome. Their intention was to connect with their Angels and Guides, but in their lack of discernment, they made contact with a lesser being that would not leave.

The key factor in this story was that they had used no protection or connection process at all. This story illustrates why some form of spiritual protection or connection is very important when working in the spiritual realms.

Where as, if you connect with Angels, Guides, Teachers, Masters, and Archangels, their glorious white light always surrounds you. Therefore you are divinely protected However, whichever approach you take it amounts to the same thing.

One day my friend Sheila asked me "Julia, how would I know when I need protection?" So I gave her this list of questions to answer.

    1   Have you ever walked into work feeling great and then within an hour felt bad or down?
    2   Do you have people who drain you of your energy?
    3   Have you ever been sucked into someone else's bad mood or energy?
    4   Can you get depressed for no apparent reason?
    5   Do you wake up in the morning feeling as if you have done ten rounds with Mohammed Ali?
    6   Does your sleep leave you listless, lethargic, and continually tired?

7 Are you always losing or misplacing things?
8 Do you go one step forward and then three steps back in situations?
9 Can you get to a certain point in relationships and then they blow up in your face?
10 Do people ever catch you totally unawares with very spiteful or hurtful remarks?

These are common situations that indicate that you are being affected by someone else's energy.

The method you use to protect yourself is as varied as nature, however I will list some simple and practical methods that you can choose from. Let it be noted that there is no right or wrong way, simply many different ways.

At this juncture I feel it is very important that together, we take a Master souls or Angels view of this subject, which is a perspective full of compassion and understanding. The closer we get to ascension the clearer we understand the fact that all souls are light, a divine spark of the Creator, and pure in essence. What will cause a soul to become "Not so Light" are its particular thoughts, motives, actions and limited understanding. It is not our task to judge anyone, but to offer hope, light, and understanding.

Connection
In my spiritual education I was never taught the concept that I had to "**protect**" myself. We were taught the principal of always tuning into or "**connecting**" with the highest spiritual sources possible. This meant the realms of the Spiritual masters like Mother Mary, Sananda (Christ), Lord Buddha, and the hosts of Angels and Archangels, rather than protecting myself from a lower source.

However I neither naïve nor ignorant about the levels of confusion that I might encounter in my healing work, and I was given a deep working knowledge of how to handle these situations. When we embrace the concept or idea that we have to protect ourselves, there is automatically the assumption that there is an adversary to protect you from.

Your intention is the key to the highest realms. If it is your intention to talk to Sanada (Christ) or any other heavenly body or being, your desire will connect you. So, the method you use to open these heavenly realms to your consciousness can change daily. There is no ritual or method that stands more important or powerful than any other, because the godhead senses your heart and intention.

So let's move on to some methods of connection. Here are the most common ones that over the years I have used in my classes and workshops around the world.

1. Saying a form of prayer like the one below, and you can substitute the word God for Angels, Christ, or I Am,
The light of GOD surrounds me/us
The Love of GOD enfolds me/us
The power of GOD protects me/us
The presence of GOD watches over me/us
Where ever I am/we are, GOD is.
2. Visualizing white /gold light surrounding you, and filling the room, house, car or place of work.
3. Putting on a cloak of deep purple/indigo and pulling the hood up over your head so that you are encased in the cloak of protection.
4. Ask Archangel Michael, Gabriel or Raphael to be by your side to assist and protect you.
5. Saying a prayer or affirmation that is very meaningful to you.

The method that has been the mainstay of my spiritual journey is the one I call "Spiritual Cleansing" or "Tuning In",

so follow the step-by-step procedure and experience it for yourself.
1. Shake your hands 2-3 times. This stimulates the healing energy in them.
2. Place the fingertips of both hands on the centre of your forehead, (your third eye), and gently draw them across your brow to your temples.
3. Shake your hands 2-3 times again to recharge them.
4. Place your fingertips of both hands back on your third eye again, lift them up over your head, touching the back of your neck, then draw them around your neck, until your fingers meet under your chin.
5. Shake your hands 2-3 times again to recharge them.
6. Repeat this whole process 3-4 times, taking deep slow breathes at the same time.
7. As you are doing this process repeat out loud, or mentally, one of the following statements.
"I am filled with God's Love"
"I am filled with peace and harmony"
"In the name of my angels, I cleanse my body and soul"
"I am divinely loved and protected"
"I am peaceful, calm and filled with grace"

You can use any positive spiritual statement that will lift your thoughts and feelings to the highest level possible. I like to vary my statement, depending on the situation and how I feel at the time.

This simple process has been known to cure Migraines, Headaches, Poor sleep patterns, and will buffer and protect you from the influence of,
    Other people's negativity.
    Being drained of energy by other people.
    Taking on other people's problems.
    Getting caught in "bad" energy.

Spiritual cleansing or tuning in will take your energy up to match that of your angels and guides, and therefore give you more energy and vitality. When you make the connection with spirit you will receive clear communication and messages from them, and it will ensure that you are always tuning into the highest source possible. You will know when you are attuned to the highest levels because you will be covered in chills or goose bumps, or suffused with love.

If you want to want walk the Ascension highway and become a master, you are the one who has to "Tune in", and become a part of the great energy force that we know as the creator, God or the great I Am. This Highway is likened to one of those "conveyor belt people movers" at airports, it is always working to move you along quicker, but you are the one who must decide whether to get on it or not.

**For he has given an
Angel in charge of thee**

Asking questions and getting Answers

Communication, in the Heavens is run by the same principles as here on Earth,
If you want clear answers, you must ask clear questions
There is no doubt that the secret to receiving clearly recognizable answers from your Angels is directly attributed to the clarity of your questions. If you are vague, broad and non-specific in the formulation of your questions, then you will find it hard to distinguish the answers. For example;
"Angels will I be happy?" Happy about what? Over what situation?
"Angels please help me be in the right place at the right time" For what, purchasing a bed at a great price? buying a car? What? What? What?

Sometimes there are underlying beliefs that are influencing how we perceive the role of our Angels, and hence, how we believe they will or can help us. Here are several common reasons for this,
1. You may be afraid to ask for things, or to bother the Universe with your trivial stuff.
2. You may think that your Angels are like fairy godmothers and that they will fix things for you or grant you every wish.
3. You may feel it is like having a Genie and a lamp and you only get three wishes, so you may be scared you are going to choose the wrong thing.
4. You may believe it is "wrong" to ask the Heavens for things.
5. You may be angry because God did not do as you requested in the past so you don't bother now.

6   You may believe that it is spiritually inappropriate to ask for "Earthly" things.
7   You may feel that you are too insignificant for the Universe to bother about.
8   You may feel that don't deserve help from Angelic beings because of your actions in the past.
9   You may feel you should be able to solve your own problems

If you are to have a clear and personal communication with the Divine you will need to grow beyond some or all of the above things that may be influencing you. After all, these are man's view of how "God and the Angels" will or will not work with you, and have no bearing in the truth of spiritual law at all.

So let's get three things clear straight away.

Firstly

Hear this! Your Angels have never ever judged any of your actions or thoughts, and never will. Evaluating your actions, decisions or attitudes past or present, is your job and no one else's. This process of gaining the wisdom from all your experiences is your personal responsibility. This is called empowerment and enlightenment, and the only reason we have experiences here on Earth.

Secondly

You are a perfect spiritual being, no less than the stars in the heavens, so why would you be of lesser importance than anyone else. As an evolving souls you are no better nor worse than anyone else, just different. You are a part of the great Oneness, love, and the energy we call the Creator so how can you be "less" than another being.

To this end, sometimes they will not get involved in something you insist upon doing, for they can see it is not for your highest good. If they can't do "good" they will not create any further harm, so they will wisely leave you to your own

choices. You will learn, what you insist upon learning. Remember that great quotation
"Fools rush in where Angels fear to tread"
Your Angels and the higher beings have always, and will continue to energise things that are for your greatest good and spiritual evolution.

Thirdly
If you feel that you have asked and asked your Angels for help in the past, and nothing has been forthcoming, then you have probably "Wanted your own way" rather than what was for your highest good. It would be wise not to "Want a specific answer" when you ask a question of your Angels, but be as detached from the situation as you possibly can. This way you can "hear" what is for your highest good in any particular situation.

I had a client who came for a reading and her opening statement to me was that she had been to 8 other psychics and they had all been wrong. I instantly "knew" that this was because she wanted to hear what "She wanted to hear" and not what her Angels may wish to tell her. I also realised that I was going to be the 9th psychic that was "wrong" for her.

If we nag or plague the universe often enough so that we get the answer we want, there will be a soul out there who will willingly give you the answer you desire. However, let it be noted that the answer may not be coming from an Angel or higher being of light. Remember, It is wise to accept that not all spiritual beings are of the highest source and wisdom, much the same as all people who are here on earth are not good, kind, loving, giving and wise. (See the chapter on Protection and Connection)

In order to receive the clearest answers to questions that you ask of your Angels, there are a few ground rules that you should follow.

1. Always use a connection or protection method to connect to the highest source available to you. (See the chapter on Protection and Connection)
2. Endeavour to be as calm and peaceful as possible.
3. Take your time when talking to your Angels. A hurried, harried or impatient energy will cloud your connection and the answers you receive.
4. If you are very emotional about a situation you will quite possibly cloud and even influence the answer you receive.
5. You need to be "unattached" to the outcome, and be willing to accept that spirits view of your highest good or life, is often much different than yours.
6. Do not ask them if you "should do this" or "should do that" as this sets them up to tell you what to do, and that is not their role. Their role is to inspire, suggest and guide you, not be one of your parents.

By using the aforementioned suggestions, you can clarify any situation that arises in your life. The less time you waste in indecision, where your energy gets depleted, the better.

Now lets address the specifics of asking questions and getting Answers.

If you are seeking an answer to a specific question using a pendulum or your body as a pendulum, then you must phrase the question so that either a "Yes" or a "No" can answer it. I have used my body as a pendulum for over 30years and love its simplicity and portability.

Using this (the pendulum) method I have been able to ask my angels questions while counselling clients, in department stores, in the car, on an aircraft, and on trains. I get an answer "on the spot" and therefore can act accordingly. I do not need special conditions nor much preparation, except to tune in of course. This means my angels are on tap to help me, at any time night or day.

So here is how can you establish and use your body as a pendulum the same as I do. Personally, I use a rocking movement, either backwards or forwards for a YES answer and a side-to-side rocking movement for a NO answer. If my body sways around in a circular motion then I know my question was not specific enough and I need to rephrase it.

1. Stand with your feet about 20 centimetres apart.
2. Rock your own body (from your ankles) forwards and backwards and mentally say "Angels this motion is to mean Yes"
3. Next, rock your own body (from your ankles) side to side and mentally say "Angels this motion is to mean No"
4. Now take a deep breath in and ask "Angels give me a Yes movement?" Exhale and wait for the movement. It should come in a couple of seconds.
5. Now take a deep breath in and ask "Angels give me a No movement?" Exhale and wait for the movement. It should come in a couple of seconds.
6. This completes the establishment of your pendulum movement. You never have to "set it up" again. Your Angels now know that they can use this method of moving your body to "Talk" to you.
7. Taking a deep breath in while you are asking the question helps you "get your own will or ego out of the way". Then, when you exhale your body relaxes and the answer, via the appropriate movement, will be there.

This method takes but seconds to do, and yet can save me hours, days, weeks, or even months of anguish and indecision.

Some of my clients can feel this same movement internally so that their body stays motionless, but they can discern the same yes/no movement inside of themselves. Many people are extremely skilled with their crystal pendulums and yet are limited to the appropriate time and place in which to use it. It is for this reason alone that I like to use my body as a pendulum.

So, armed with this tool, it still comes back to the clearest answers will be received if you ask clear questions. Remember you are only ever asking the light realms for their opinion of your situation. You are asking them to help you make the wisest decision possible, not to actually make the decision for you. Therefore, your questions must be phrased as a request of their view, perspective and opinion of the wisest way forward in any given situation.
For example;

    a. Is it in my best interests to blah blah…………………………
    b. Is this the best time for me to blah blah……………………
    c. Is blah blah blah the best solution to the following situation
    d. Which month is the wisest time for me to do blah blah……
    (This can be applied to any time frame e.g. week, month or year)
    e. If you were in my shoes Angels, would you blah blah……..
    f. Is it part of my life purpose to blah blah …………………….

Obviously, the blah, blah, blah, is the space where you would insert the question you specifically wanted answered.
I particularly use example b. and d. a lot, because I like to find myself in the right place at the right time to meet people, present a workshop, have a holiday or take work opportunities. I also use this when I am planning to buy an expensive item such as a piece of furniture. In the past, I have been impatient and then find the item I bought went on sale just 4 days after I purchased it. Grrrr.

If I really get stuck I will use example e. and f. This is a good way of determining if I am being a fool and rushing in where they would fear to tread. If my Angels would not do something I am contemplating doing, then there is no way on heaven or earth I would do it either.

Once again, using the pendulum method, you can clarify what your sensitivity perceives. How often have you dismissed an insight or feeling because you convinced yourself you must have been imagining things? Have you ever questioned whether something was your thought or an insight from your Angels? This particularly happens when your Angels are communicating to you through the gift of mental telepathy. Now if you get a message and you are not sure whether to give it credibility or not, you can ask,
Angels, did you just give me the insight to blah blah ....

One day, after a lovely lunch, I was actually writing this very chapter, when I had to stop and go to the local store for some groceries. Walking up the driveway my stomach suddenly felt very bloated, painful and very uncomfortable. It made no sense that I felt this way, and yet it was like a huge wave of pain and stomach dissention had overcome me. I stopped and asked my angels, "Is this feeling mine?" and the answer was a very clear "No". So I proceeded to the store to make my purchases and then returned home. Later that day I was to find out that a friend had just been diagnosed with ovarian cancer, and the mass was causing her to have a very painful, bloated and distended stomach. Unconsciously, I was tuning in to her and feeling her pain and discomfort.

Asking your Angels "Is this headache mine? Are these confusing thoughts mine? I am feeing very depressed today Angels, are these feelings mine? (90% of the time they will not be yours) I think you will me amazed to discover how sensitive you are to the thoughts, emotions and feelings of other people. This will be true at home, at work and even socially.

The following method is excellent for determining whether the thoughts or feeling you are experiencing are yours or not. Angels, to what % are these feelings of confusion, depression or doubt that I am experiencing, mine
    100%..."No".
    90%...."No".
    80%...."No".
    70%...."No".
    and keep going until you receive a yes answer.

Much of the time you will find that the negative feelings you experience are not yours. Personally, I am never interested in whose feelings they are, as long as I know they aren't mine, I can dismiss them. If they aren't mine, why would I want to waste time and energy on them?

If you are constantly asking the universe questions for help, without ever taking time to listen for the reply, you will not hear the response. Your mind chatter won't let a light being get a word in edgeways. Have you ever spoken to a person who talks all the time, without ever listening to your replies.

They ignore you and continue chattering even when you try to say something. When I am trying to communicate with someone like this, I eventually have to disconnect or disengage from him or her. It is no different when you are communicating with your Angels, light beings or god.
The Universe will be forced to metaphorically put the receiver down on you if you do not stop talking and asking, and begin to listen. This is the reason it is called "Communicating (two way) with Angels", not "Talking to Angels"

It's a good practice to take 1-2 minutes several times a day to tune in and actually ask, "Angels is there anything you want to tell me?" I do this by stopping, standing or sitting still, I then take a deep breath and as I exhale I ask the question. If all remains silent then I carry on with my tasks and activities.

Meditation

This is a great method for listening to the voice of God/Creator/the Universe. It necessitates you being able to put yourself away from the hustle and bustle of life in order to hear the still quiet voice of the Divine.

You can also use Meditation to restore your inner peace and calm, your energy levels and relax your physical body. It could be considered a "Green" or natural prescription for holistic health and well-being.

The aim and intention of meditation is to still our chattering minds (I call it having a Monkey Mind) long enough for the Divine to drop seeds of guidance or wisdom into our conscious awareness. There are people, of which I am one, who find it very difficult to meditate formally as a person from an eastern philosophy might do.

I find my still moments come when I am gardening, sitting near water, or when taking a walk in nature. Others find that at creative times such as when they are painting, sewing, playing music, doing woodturning, carving, or doing pottery. The mind chatter ceases and the right brain is then open to receive inspiration. Any activity that allows your mind to empty for a time, be it a moment or an hour, is considered a form of meditation.

Some of us will feel better dedicating longer slices of time to this way of communing with the universe, and others will do it in shorter spans and more often. Whether you devote long periods of time to connect with your spiritual source or to do it frequently is a personal choice. It in no way reflects the quality of connection you can establish with Angelic beings. There are also many ways to pray or meditate to connect with that same source. Each to our own.

Writing a letter to God/Universe or your Angels

You can write down you problem or dilemma on a piece of writing paper and then put it in a book or place that is sacred or a place that is meaningful to you. As you place it in this "special" place you ask to be divinely guided to do what is for the highest good of all concerned about the situation. Then forget it, let it go, yes, let it go and see what happens.

Personally, I like to put my piece of paper in a plastic bag and place it in the kitchen freezer. Now that I have frozen my problem I let it go and let the universe take care of it. Sometimes the situation gets solved and I have had to do nothing. At other times I will, after a period of time, be guided as to what is the best thing for me to do.

Sometimes we commit something to God or the universe to attend to, and then we take the situation back and try to do it our selves again. There is absolutely no point in asking for divine help if you are not willing to give the problem over to God for its insight and answer. You need to trust, trust, trust.

It was my dear friend Janette, who illustrated the best analogy about trust I have ever heard. She says it is like posting a letter.
If you are strong in the quality of trust you put the letter in the post box and never consider that it would not reach its destination.
If you are weak in trust, you would put it in the post box, then sit there and wait for the mail man to collect it, then you would follow him to the sorting office to make sure it gets sorted properly, then follow the intercity truck to ensure it gets to the right city and so on, until it is delivered.

I discovered this delightful message in a book and have passed it on to clients, and workshop participants. It is a very light-hearted piece that possibly sums up how the universe might feel about helping to solve our problems.

A Message from God

Listen-Up, I am God! And today I will be handling all your problems.
Please remember I do not need your help.
If life happens to deliver a situation that you can't handle, do not attempt to resolve it.
Kindly put it in the SFGTD (Something for God to do) box.
It will be addressed in my time, not yours.
Once the matter is placed into the box, do not hold on to it (in your mind) or remove it. Holding on or the removal of it will only delay the resolution of your problem.
If it is situation that you think you are capable of handling, please consult me to be sure that it is the proper course of action.
Because I do not sleep or slumber, there is no need for you to lose any sleep over the matter.
Rest, and if you should need to contact me, I am only a thought or prayer away.

After reading this, many of us got busy and created, then filled, our "Something for God to do" boxes.

Because of their commitment to you, your Angels will help and guide you in every facet of your life. For example they will assist you with,

Relationships	Money & Finances
Education	Career
Vacations	Purchasing items
Recreational pursuits	Health

and finally, the Manifesting your Dreams & Wishes.
Everything in your life, whether small or big can be assisted by angels, that is as long as it is for your highest good.

Having read this chapter you will have noticed I am a "No Frills" person when it comes to communicating with my Angels. There are,
no flowers   no fancy notepaper   no crystals   no candles and no special rituals or settings.

You may want do these things, and your Angels will appreciate the sentiment behind such acts. However, they are not needed, nor necessary, for you to enjoy a very clear two-way communication with the heavens. Communicating with your Angels is actually as natural as breathing and as portable as walking. If fact, it's quite un-natural, for you not to have a clear communication with the universal light beings.

**A man does not have to be an Angel
in order to be a saint**

Why we "appear" get wrong answers

When you are asking the universe questions about a situation that involves another person, or several other people, what they tell you and what actually happens can be different. This can be very disappointing and may even lead you to doubt your angels or your connection with them.

When you are asking about a situation that involves another person, you have to take into account that they have free will. People can, and at times will, change their mind about a situation. The best way to illustrate this concept is with an example.

A friend was separated from her husband and after much discussion they agreed to reunite and set about making their marriage work. She felt very strongly that everything was going to work out fine, and yet when she asked her angels whether they thought the reconciliation was in her best interests they said "No". No matter how she phrased the question, it still came back as "No".

However she decided to trust her own good feelings about the situation and return home. She was only there 24 hours when her husband received a call from the hospital where his ex girlfriend had just been admitted after a serious suicide attempt. The girlfriend was sobbing on the phone and wanted him to come to her side immediately. Faced with his drama the husband said to his wife'

"You're tough, you're strong, you will have to go, I will have to go to her, as she needs me". Within an hour, my friend was unceremoniously bundled out of the house with her marriage irreversibly shattered. When she was calm enough to review the situation with me, we looked at why her feelings told her one thing and her Angels suggested another.

Her Angels told her that from her point of view she could have made the marriage work. This statement supported her feelings.

However, her angels could see the bigger picture, which included the emotionally unstable ex girlfriend and the influence she would exert on the situation. They could foresee that the reconciliation situation was not going to be for my friends highest emotional and spiritual good.

In this instance where you have feelings that indicate one direction, and your angels suggest another, I suggest you ask them this question. "Angels can you see something about this situation that I cannot?" If the answer is yes, then you know that they are guiding you so as to prevent you wasting, time, energy, and money, or saving you emotional pain and mental anguish.

A client was house hunting and eventually came across what she thought was her perfect house. Her heart told her this was the place and she asked her angels "Will I get this house?" and she felt the answer was yes. She asked her angels what they felt was the "best" offer for her to make with the view to being the successful buyer, and they told her the amount. So she promptly tendered a price that was above the current valuation and yet remained within her budget, and awaited the outcome. She was absolutely devastated when the real estate agent informed her, that she was not the successful purchaser. She immediately felt very upset at her angels because she felt they had given her the wrong information and therefore misled her.

When we reviewed the situation together several things came to light.
1. She never asked her Angels did they have another property that was even more appropriate for her. Even if she did not think that it would be possible.
2. She never asked if it was in her best interests to continue looking at other houses.

3. She never asked if it was likely that another prospective buyer would offer a higher price.
4. She never asked if this was the most appropriate or perfect timing to buy a buy a house. She assumed it was.
5. She never even considered that another buyer might offer a higher price AFTER her bid was tendered.
6. She never asked her angels if it would be wise to be prepared to be disappointed or trust that what ever happens if therefore "the best thing": even if she cannot see why at the time.

When we are taking action on a situation that involves other people there really can never be any absolutes. Why? Because other people have free will and their actions can, at any time, influence our prospective outcomes.

Another client had two children went to the same school. Her son, then aged nine, was having difficulties with his academic progress. This caused his Mum a great deal of worry. So she set about asking her Angels for guidance.
Using the pendulum method (as detailed in the chapter on Asking questions and getting Answers) she had asked her angels if she should move her children to another school. The answer she got was not clear. In fact every time she asked she seemed to get conflicting answers, so she finally spoke to me about what was the best thing to do for her children.
Upon questioning her, we discovered that there were actually a numbers of questions that needed to be posed to her angels, in order to receive a clear response. Because the situation was unclear in her mind, how could she ever expect a clear response?
For example
    1. She was only worried about her son, and yet was asking her Angels about moving both children to another school.
    2. She assumed her son's educational performance was paramount at the tender age of nine.

3. She gave no consideration to the children being happy at school and as we know if they are happy, they learn better.

When we defined these things she found out that her son's angels were focusing on him learning social skills as his current priority. They felt there was time enough for him to focus on his ABC's. Also, she was able to ask her Angels if the school he was in was the best for his growth at this time. Her daughter actually never even featured in the situation.

In my experience you cannot ask your Angels for answers or information about **another persons**' possible actions or choices, and expect to get answers from the highest light sources. Why? Because what you are asking is probably none of your business.

However as with all rules, there are exceptions. These are
- If you are doing spiritual readings or consultations for a person. If you are then that person has, by their very presence, given you permission to glimpse their pathway.
- If you are the parent of small children. Your children's Angels will assist you with insights into their needs in the areas of health, education, and emotional well-being. The greatest amount of assistance you will get will be from birth until 4 years of age. Around this time the little "old soul" will start to find its own sense of self and confidence. The insights you get from their Angels will dwindle until the age of 14 when they are deemed, with guidance, to be able to make decisions for themselves.
- If you are a carer (medical, spiritual, emotional or physical) of a person who is seriously or terminally ill.

At this time the universe feels it is very apt to guide someone to assist the sick person in the most appropriate manner.

There will be situations when you feel it is the right time to get insights and answers to a situation, and yet the universe will feel it is not the appropriate time to do so. At these times we are learning the wisdom of "The Mysteries of the Universe".

In one dialogue I had with my Angels, they said to me
"Julia, if we told you all there is to know, then you would never experience the wonder of the mysteries and magic of the universe. Also, what you need to know in one moment is very different from what you need to know in the next, depending on your thoughts and actions. Rest assured when you need to know something we will make sure you receive the information".

It is said that a wise person;
Knows they don't know
Therefore, wisely accepts that at this time they don't need to know
For they know, that when they need to know,
They will know

Actually, sometimes knowing things can be a burden.

A client asked me how her very sick husband was doing. She was terrified that he might pass on because she was so frightened of living without him. When I tuned in, his Angels told me that he was going to pass on soon, but I was to say that he was going to be just fine. She was not to worry or fret about him, but to enjoy him.
Four weeks later she rang me up and was very angry with me indeed. It seemed her husband had passed on and I was to blame, as I had told her he would be fine. Fortunately, I knew how deep and raw her grief was, so I let her vent some of her anger on me. I offered her a refund of the fee she had paid and she readily accepted. So I promptly sent her a sympathy card and popped the refund cheque inside it.

Two months later I got the most beautiful card from her saying how much she appreciated receiving the cheque. She added comments about how my column had been sustaining her spiritually since her husband had passed on. She apologised for being rude to me and asked if I could find it in my heart to forgive her. She added that she was slowly coping with the day-to-day things and was very comforted because she could feel the spiritual presence of her husband.

Now! I ask you? How could I, or any Angel, tell her that her husband was going to pass on when they knew how aggrieved and devastated she was going to be? It was information that she did not need to know.
She would have to cope with this soon enough. Also from the Universe's point of view he was fine, perfectly fine. He may be going to leave his physical form, but he was just fine.
As to my giving her a refund, well that was my call. I certainly did not have to, yet I rather felt from a big picture point of view it would be a wise and compassionate thing to do. In hindsight, I am so glad I took such a course of action.
In summary the main reasons we appear to get wrong answers are,
- You actually don't need to know about the situation at this time.
- You have more growth to do before certain insights will be available.
- There are more than one person/persons influencing the situation.

- In an act of compassion the universe will not give you the insight you seek.
- There is a much bigger picture afoot and you are thinking to small.
- You are not being open or flexible enough to see a wider view.

- You need to "live in the now" over the matter
- You are not defining the situation clearly enough
- You are not asking enough questions about the situation

**If you must keep company,
make sure it includes
the company of Angels**

Asking Cupid for a life partner

Many of us put more time and effort into choosing a new car than we do into the choosing of a life partner. In this day and age we are taught to be very goal and achievement oriented about our careers, purchasing a house, and planning our vacations, yet we happily leave the finding of a partner to "chance". Would it not follow, and make sense, to put a little time into the planning and deciding about what we truly require in a relationship? That way we might be more successful in our choice of partners.

Your Angels and Cupid certainly think so. It is not enough to tell them that you want someone to be happy with, because each of us, at any given time, is as happy or sad as we decide to be. Also, along the same line of thought, our happiness is our responsibility and so it is unfair to charge someone else with that task.

The angels that take care of romance and love relationships, ironically, are actually the group of angels called cupids. Their sole purpose is to connect the people that have a sacred contract to be together as a couple, at the appropriate time. They "live" to bring love into bloom between people when the universal timing is right.

It may be that you have several "love" contracts, each with a different aspect of love for you to experience. Conversely, I know people who met their prospective partners as early as at primary school and others who knew they would marry their high school sweetheart. Having one partner for 35 years, or having several loves in your life is neither right nor wrong, it is simply different.

I remember one relationship of mine that lasted only 19months, and yet it was to be the foundation upon which I assessed all the relationships that followed. Until I met Michael* I didn't really know what I wanted in a partner. Nor did I realize that I deserved so much more than I had been accepting, up until the time I met him. He was my prototype of the perfect or ideal partner to share my life with.

His purpose in entering my life was solely to give me an example of how life could be with an appropriate partner. He was my friend, my lover, my confidante, and above all else, he filled my life with the joy of doing things together, in a way I had never known until that time.

He passed on in 1991, just14 months after we stopped seeing each other and I have missed him every week since that time. On several occasions he has taken the time to contact me through spiritual mediums and my dreams. The most recent contact was the most poignant; as I know it will be our final contact in this time space. We finally were ready to regroup what we both gained mentally, emotionally and spiritually from the time we had spent together. At last we are both at peace from the experience.

* Not his real name

It was my experience with him that gave rise to the technique that follows on how to attract the most appropriate person for you to spend some rich emotionally, mentally and spiritually time with. Bearing in mind, that for some of us, this connection may take place in your twenties or thirties and for some of us it may not take place until much later in life.

You will notice that I have made no reference to the much abused, term your "Soul Mate". Why? Because you're Mum, Dad, siblings, friends of the same and opposite sex, and some people at work are all your soul mates. Souls mates are people with whom you have a special affinity. You have a connection that can be felt immediately when you meet them.

I have done a great deal of counselling with people who were attracted and connected to a person and believed they had found their "soul Mate". Time soon revealed that this was not the case and my clients were truly shattered about how the relationship had all gone sour. Many of these connections and subsequent associations, are past life ties that are not meant to be "re lived" this lifetime, and so must inevitably end. Or, it can even be that you had one final experience to have with that person to complete a past life contact, and once it is done, the relationship will come to an end.

Spiritually, it is much healthier to make a list based on what you need, want, and desire and offer it up into the hands of your Angels to manifest in a timing that is perfect for you.

In order to enlist your angels and cupids assistance with finding a wonderfully appropriate person for you, you have to clarify what "**YOU**" **want and need**. This is your part of the deal or request, and of course this will be much different for a person in there twenties than a person in the fifties. If you do not know what you need and want, it is highly unlikely that your prospective partner, no matter how psychic, will know.
Having done this step, you can now turn to what you would like in a partner. Once you have put down on paper the kind of person you want and need, they will go ahead and arrange for circumstances to coincide so that two of you can meet. So let us begin.

The first step is to know the qualities and attributes you would like your ideal partner to have. In a way it is rather like shopping, you have to know what you want to purchase before you can recognize the correct product. It is in this category you itemise qualities like honesty, good communication skills, sense of humour, spontaneity, a person free of addictions, consideration, patience, willing to resolve difficulties etc.

If you know what you "don't want", then study this quality and find one that is the exact opposite. If you write down "I don't want a gambler" the universe does not recognise the word "Not" and so they send you a gambler. The same as if you write down "I don't want a man who doesn't respect me" the universe will not recognise the word don't and so you will attract a man who treats you with disrespect.

Secondly, you can ask for preferred physical attributes, but don't get too hung up about them, for often the most appropriate person may come wrapped in a different parcel than the one you were looking or hoping for.

Because I am a little on the ample in size, (reubenesque) would be a good description), I always wanted a man that was 6ft 2 inches plus in height, so that I would appear petite, feminine, and ladylike beside him. Did I ever attract a man this tall? No chance, because I had to learn to like and accept myself as I am.

Do you want a partner that is sexually active and to what level? What sort of image would you like e.g. A snappy dresser in a suit, or a casual outdoors sporty type, or a sports person and fan, a homely family type person. Would they be required to be at your side at a business function as an asset to your job or profession?

My daughter always gave me heaps about the fact that I require a person with good table manners and etiquette. She feels I am being judgmental and too much of a perfectionist. However it's important to me and personally, I simply could not spend years sitting at the dining table with someone who lacked pleasant, socially acceptable table manners.
Do you need someone who is mentally stimulating and interesting?

Lastly, you need to define why you want your long-term partner.
- Is it for the purpose of raising children together?
- Is companionship the highest priority?
- Would you like to do things together?
- Do you want to mutually help each other be the best they can be?
- Do you want your partner to bring a more social life into the relationship?
- Do you require time and space to maintain your individual hobbies and pursuits?
- Would you like someone interested in travel, cultures and exotic foods to have experiences with?
- Do you want your partner to be spiritually aligned with your religion or beliefs?

If you are a great fan of watching and going to the movies or theatre do you want someone who shares these interests. If you have children from a previous marriage or relationship, I image you will want to specify that your ideal partner fits in well with your existing family.

Having answered all these questions and really thought about the person you would like to experience a relationship with, you are ready to make a **Love Magnet.**
Begin with a piece of paper and make out the list of the qualities, attributes, and strengths you would like your ideal partner to have. Then add the skills, be they physical, sporting, or social, and finally add any special requests. The final outcome may read something like this;

My Partner/ My Love
1. Is honest
2. Respects themselves and others
3. Is intelligent and mentally stimulating and interesting
4. Has a good sense of humour

5. Has good social skills and graces
6. Likes us doing things together
7. Will respect and support me in my career as I in theirs
8. Brings with them a social circle of friends to enjoy
9. Has their own hobbies and interests
10. Is willing to listen too, and resolve difficulties
11. Is ready and willing to be committed to a relationship
12. Is single or divorced
13. Has regrouped their past relationships and is ready for a new one
14. Is well groomed and has a good sense of clothing style
15. Someone who wants to spend time with me as much as I do them
16. Loves to dance
17. Is interested in travelling overseas for holidays
18. Has spent time living alone and is capable of looking after themselves
19. Has their own hobbies and interests
20. And I can have an active, satisfying sex life
21. And I have common interests and goals
22. They demonstrate thru acts and gifts that I am very special to them
23. Their family welcome and accept me as their partner
24. Financially they are wise with their use of money
25. Is 5 foot 11 inches tall or taller
26. No more than 15 kilos over their ideal body weight
27. Is respectful of my spiritual beliefs
28. Is someone who is comfortable expressing their love and feelings
29. Enjoys the movies, arts and theatre
30. The person must be male or female. (this tip comes from someone who met the perfect partner with one catch. The person was of the same sex, which is not what my client wanted)

The moment your list is complete your angels and cupid start doing what they need to do to have this person manifest in your life. You can choose to put your list in your diary, a special significant spiritual book, or paste it onto a sheet of cardboard to place on the inside of your wardrobe door. If you want to adorn your page with pictures of angels, wedding rings, or any other his and her items it will all add to the strength and power the **Love Magnet** will have.

Now your angels really have something to work with. How they will go about the fulfilment of your list is an interesting journey in itself. You may need to do some inner work and make some changes in order to be the kind of person that your "Dream Person" will be attracted to. It's no good looking for the handsome knight in shining armour that is seeking a princess or maiden, if you are standing at the roadside dresses in jeans and a tee shirt.

So, they may guide you to
- Loose weight
- Take on a fitness programme
- Start classes in dancing
- Read books about relationships
- Have a "clean up and clean out" session at home
- Start a new hobby or interest
- Take up further education
- Develop more spiritually
- Have some coaching or counselling sessions
- Have a wardrobe, image or beauty makeover
- Do some travelling
- Change your job
- Learn to play bridge
- Join a community service club
- To start your own business

All these activities are in order to increase your desirability and prepare you for meeting your new partner. The suggestion I make to my family, friends and class participants, is that they make themselves into the kind of person they would love to spend the rest of their lives with.

Do not be surprised, when you go out socially, if no-one of the opposite sex speaks or interacts with you. There is nothing wrong with you, it is just that the universe is filtering people and diverting those people who would not be appropriate for you. This is, after all, what you have asked them to do.

Finally, do not loose heart. You may not connect with your "special person" this year, or even the next, but they will arrive, often when you least expect it. But rest assured, it will be in the perfect Universal or Gods timing, not one moment sooner or later.

In the relationship quest, there are some pitfalls that people can fall into. I am constantly amazed at the number of people who have come to me seeking information from the universe about when will "their perfect love" come along, while they are still in their current relationship. They may be unhappy in their marriage or with the partner they are committed to, and before they have even ended it, they are looking for the next partner.

This is a sign of spiritual immaturity. How can we possibly be ready for a new partnership when we haven't even gone through all the growth that comes from ending the current one? The answer is we can't, which is probably why "rebound" unions do not work. Moving from one relationship to the next does not give you the space to discover things like,

> What have I gained from this partnership?
> How have I grown as a soul?
> What do I know about myself now that I did not know before?
> Where do I need to change?
> What is it I really want now?
> What are my personal needs?
> Do I need to respect myself more?

How can I improve my communication?
Do I need to clearly state my needs and wants right up front?
What am I afraid of, if anything?
Based on my past what do I want in a new relationship?

Until we know what we need and want ourselves, how can we expect another person to know. If we place this burden of responsibility on another person then we are being a child and making them the parent. In as much as you assume they will take care of you and do the right thing for you and by you.

If it hurts it isn't love. Many folks are enduring unions with partners who hurt them,
    Mentally   Emotionally
    Spiritually   Physically
and then declare that this abusive partner loves them. When I enquire as to what it is that makes them say their partner loves them, they reply;
"Because he/she says they do". This is what their partner declares, especially after a bout of abuse. These hurtful actions, by any individual, are not actions of someone who loves their partner or children. It is by a person's actions that we really know them, not by what they say. This form of abusive behaviour is actually based on fear. And at the risk of oversimplifying a complex set of behaviours, it is usually because the "Bully" is terrified the person they care about will leave them for someone else.

The spiritual growth in these kinds of unions is not about being loved and cherished but rather things like;
    Reclaiming your personal identity
    Reclaiming your personal energy and power
    Exercising your right to make decisions
    Exercising your personal freedom

> Standing up for your beliefs and values
> Choosing to live without fear
> Starting anew, despite the past
> Trusting the universe will provide for you
> Believing in yourself and your own abilities

You may have expected your relationship to bring you love and yet sadly, it did not. I feel this is a great part of the pain we feel when partnerships end. Yet, if we looked back, did we define the growth or the type of person we wanted to practice the joys of love with. Or, typically, did we expect that being in a partnership this would automatically happen.

It is not wrong to have expectations, it's just that you need to define what they are, and then communicate them. They can be things like,

> Agreeing on whether or not to have children.
> Fostering children.
> Accepting an infirmed parent/child living in the house.
> Being prepared to live in the country of your birth.
> Financial security.
> Agreeing to a pre-nuptial agreement.
> Having a big church wedding.
> Not actually ever getting married.

So, now you can see why all the inner work to create the relationship you truly desire is worth the effort. By seeking the answers to what you need and want, making your list of your ideal partner, and then, finally, creating your "love magnet", you will have done "your share" of the effort required to manifest your special person. Now your Angels will assist the cupids to bring you experiences that will be about love, as well as being for your highest good.

Be assured the universe runs on love, it thrives on love, and you are love. If you want to be loved, give it to others. Share all manner of loving things, thoughts, acts and kindness's to the people around you and it will come back to you in unlimited quantities. You will be a most loved child of the universe.

**Remember
Love, loves love**

Letting go and Letting God

This is probably one of the hardest universal laws to live while we are here on earth. Which is the reason why it is one of the highest spiritual laws. It takes a great degree of "surrender and trust" to let the Godhead decide what is best for you. This is especially true if we have pre-determined ideas about what we came to experience this lifetime. Lets look at the most common example of this to illustrate my point, relationships.

We live in a world that is fundamentally based on the family unit and interpersonal relationships. However this does not necessarily mean that we all came to gain our major growth from this facet of life. It certainly will appear that this may be case, because the myth that is perpetuated is that of "Man meets Woman" and they live happily ever after. This fairy story tells us that if we meet Mr or Miss "right" we will be blissfully happy and our partner will be the source of all our joy. So! You may well ask, why is this man/woman stuff a myth? Well, the answer lies in the spiritual laws.

Spiritually, we know that no one person outside of ourselves can make us happy. Also! No one outside ourselves is responsible for making us happy. At any given time, each one of us is as happy as we choose and allow ourselves to be.

While marriage or committed relationships is definitely a major aspect of growth for many souls, it is not the path for us all. So then! If you have a fixed view that your path is about relationships and having a partner, you can be severely hindering your own growth. Not only that, you will end up very, very disappointed when "it does not happen for you". Or, worse still, you could spend your whole life looking for "your partner" and feel hollow, empty and unfulfilled for years.

Therefore my suggestion to you about this man/woman myth is to "let it go". Open your mind to the possibility that you came to experience other deep and meaningful things as well as relationships. Look further, broader, wider and higher to see where else you are being called or drawn too. Rest assured, if your major growth is to come about through a partnership, it will. You need to trust that the godhead will and can, bring it about in the divine and perfect time, and only when you are spiritually ready.

Anne was a physically and spiritually beautiful young woman yet she was in a very unsupportive, restrictive marriage. She longed to be loved, respected and cherished by a partner.
So much so, that she fell prey to affection outside of her marriage. This lovely eligible man Anne was having a friendship with, then went on to meet a single woman and began a serious relationship with her. Anne was so distressed as she had wanted the gentleman to rescue her from her unhappy situation. Her every conversation was full of either diminishing her husband and bemoaning his failings, or praising her man friend. She was hanging on to her outdated marriage partner, while desperately clutching to her newfound friend.
I ask you, how can her Angels or the universe possibly assist her to sort out her life, if her head and time is filled with comparative dialogues about two men. Her thoughts are manifesting a very confused life and time space for her. The problem is, of course, she is looking for love in all the wrong places.
The only way she can ever possibly be loved and nurtured in the way she desire,s is to do these things to and for herself. This would be a great part of her taking responsibility for her

own life and her emotional, mental and spiritual well-being. Then and only then, will the universe bring her a spiritually loving and appropriate partner? That is assuming relationships are a major aspect of her spiritual plan this lifetime. She needs to "Let go of her obsession with men and relationships" and let God guide her to a path of attaining her own inner happiness.

I have had many clients who are unwilling to "Let Go" of a current unfulfilling relationship until spirit brings them the new one. I feel this is rather like a monkey who is holding in each hand, a branch from two different trees. At what point does he let go so he can move on? You cannot move on until you let go of something. As the old saying goes eventually, "Somethin's gotta give".

In my observations (about the above situation) the person usually attracts another man just like the last one. They may look different, smell different, dress different but invariably, given time, they will be the same as their last partner. If you do not let go of something that no longer serves your highest good, how can something better, improved and more suitable enter into your life?

Mary was overjoyed when she met up with a child hood sweetheart. They both had been married and were now divorced. The flame they had when they were teenagers was rekindled and the relationship quickly grew into a live-in one. They got engaged and went on to discuss marriage. Yet every time wedding plans were on the table, there was always a reason why they did not suit her fiancé. After seven years, he left her for another woman.

Mary was naturally devastated. Her grief and loss about the failed relationship was almost unbearable. Time passed. She kept declaring that she was over him and moving on, and yet her old flame centred in every

conversation. How he treated her, what he said, trying to analyse things he said, second guessing what he meant, imagining what he was doing now with his new partner etc, etc, etc.
She so desperately wanted a life which included a loving partner that she had readings every 3 months to be re-assured that she "will" meet her special man. Her dream was that he would come into her life, fill it with love, blessings, and financial security and therefore make her life complete. On the other hand, she also longs to be told that she and her old flame will be reconciled and that they were really meant to be together after all. A large part of her Mary's time and energy is consumed with the subject of relationships. She is absolutely convinced that a partnership is a huge part of her plan this lifetime.

This is clearly a case of someone imposing their fixed view of what their life is supposed to be all about, rather than letting go and letting God bring forth what is for her highest good. I am not saying that a relationship is not a part of this loving woman's life plan, rather I am saying she would be wise to give up her obsession about her love life and allow God to bring to her what is for her highest good when the universal timing is right.

So then, how does a person reconcile the fact that we should set our own goals and direction and yet still "let go and let God?" How can we do take responsibility for our own life and direction and yet still practice the law of "letting go and letting God"? Well, that is what makes this situation such a delicious paradox.

There is such a fine balance to be defined between,
1. Setting your own goals, dreams and direction
2. Being personally responsible
3. And letting the universe reveal your highest good.

The best balance is to set one or several things in motion as goals and dreams and then be guided by spirit.

Do what you can, with honesty and maturity and without stress, and then let the universe do the rest. If things are not moving or changing as you thought they might or hoped they would, then look at how you may be "Holding On" to something, and therefore hindering the progress of new things manifesting. You may not be at all, which is great, because then it is a pure and simple matter of timing.

If you do this simple little self-questionnaire you will see what I mean. Take a minute to review each one and you may be surprised at what your Angels will reveal to you. The purpose is to find subtle ways that you may have become set in your perspective beliefs, concepts or actions about,

Your expectations of a situation or facet of your life.
Your view of your perfect timing.
What you deem to be your life plan.
Outdated people and relationships.
Loved ones who have passed on.
Your fixed view of how things should be.
What your definition of how your life is supposed to be.
How you should be living your life or what you should be doing.
Things you have outgrown and no longer serve your life style.

I knew a working couple whose grownup children had long since left home. They were enjoying a time when they could use their incomes for things they wanted, rather than having to always focus on the necessities like they had too in the past. They indulged in hobbies long dreamed off, one of which was photography. So, as the husband's photographic skill levels grew, so did his desire for better equipment and tools. This ultimately led to the attic containing boxes of outdated cameras, flash units, tripods, bags, books, and other things.

We were all discussing the possibility of a holiday together, and he declared that much as he would really love to go it was out of their financial reach for the foreseeable future. When I suggested that perhaps they could sell all the unused stored photographic items in the attic to pay for their trip I was unprepared for the extreme emotional response. There was "NO WAY" they were prepared to let go of those items, even though they had not used them for many years.

Often we hold onto things that no longer serve us. We do not use theses items, and they can even deteriorate by storing them. Yet, if sold, they would make wonderful
 Xmas or birthday presents for people with limited budgets, which could not afford to buy the item new. Regularly, our current dreams and wishes are hindered or even withheld, because we are not willing to "Let Go". If we let go of outdated things we create a vacuum and then the universe will rush to fill that space with something that is much more appropriate.

During my time as a counsellor I have met countless people who have, for many years, had a dream of having a spiritual centre. A special place where people can come to receive healings, treatments, readings, or even partake in a workshop. Their vision is to create a "sanctuary and retreat" where people can go to find peace, calm and spirituality. They envisage ascetically pleasing communal and accommodation buildings, set in acres of lush green grass and trees. They live for the day when they will win the lottery to be able to bring the dream into reality. From their point of view this is their personal spiritual mission, because it was an image they received from the universe.
Now! No matter what country in the world you live in, you are talking serious money to make such a vision a reality. However, these people have a fixed view of how this sanctuary can and should be created, and they are not willing to see it any other way. And what's even sadder, is the fact

that most of them will probably go to their passing believing they never achieved what they were asked to do.
When I suggest that perhaps there is another way that this dream can be interpreted and created without the actual purchase of the land and buildings I usually get a serious, I mean a very serious reaction and degree of resistance.

They are not willing to let go of their fixed interpretation of the dream. They have not, in all those intervening years once asked the universe things like;
- Is there still a need for this kind of sanctuary?
- Is this vision still relevant for my life plan?
- Was I holding the light for this vision for another person to create?
- Collectively, have we evolved past the need for such a sanctuary?
- Are you specifically asking me to build such a complex?
- Shall I find a group of other people who hold the same dream so we can create it together?

You see, often spirit asks many thousands of people to hold onto "a dream" so that the light is held for that vision. Then in the right time and place, the right people with the money and ability are able to materialise this vision quest. The catch is that because they received the vision, they never questioned if they were supposed to act on it or not.
They were not aware that they were but one of thousands, perhaps many thousands of other people worldwide, who were holding the same dream. They never thought to ask questions like,
"Can I let this dream go God?"
"Do you want me to personally act on this inspiration God?"
"God are you asking me personally to be responsible for the manifesting of this dream?"

Nowadays, versions of these sanctuaries can be seen in such forms as;
> *Beauty spas and retreats*
> *Mind Body Spirit festivals*
> *Spiritual/Psychic fairs*
> *Nature walks*
> *Venues where spiritual workshops and talks are done*
> *Peoples homes where weekly development classes are held*
> *Halls and venues where personal growth seminars are held*
> *Ocean liner cruises with spirituality as its theme*
> *Spiritualist church services*
> *Crystal shops and spiritual bookstores*

All of these above examples could all be accurately described as a healing centre or place for people to come and receive spiritual nourishment. It's in the personal interpretation, perspective or view that the difference lies.
So! Sometimes we need to let go of how we interpret things. Or, we need to check in with spirit and review the dream we hold, to clarify if it is still accurate and current in the form that we see it.

Marianne was a single Mum and was obsessed about having another baby. She was in her late 30's and to her, her body clock sounded like a time bomb. When I asked her did she want a partner, she replied by saying she wanted a baby. So I said "If it's a baby you want that's easy, your doctor can help you find a suitable sperm donor to create just the sort of child you want". Her reaction was one of horror.

I asked her once again did she want a partner or a baby? She looked very confused and flustered and then said snappily, "Of course I want a man, a man who will give me a baby"

It was at this point in our conversation it became very clear to me that she really hadn't thought through her desires clearly.

She had not decided if she wanted a life partner with whom, through their shared love for one another, a child would be created. The only thing that was clear was she wanted a baby.

Clearly, if she did not change her thinking, she was probably going to attract a man who would get her pregnant and then as likely as not, desert her. Then she would be left resentful that he did not take on an active role in the child's rearing.

However, she would be manifesting exactly the confused situation that her thoughts were creating. She would have been very wise to investigate why she was so obsessed about having another child. Why? Because obsession, by its very nature of possessive attachment, is not for anyone's highest good. It is actually a contravention of the spiritual laws.

I even have an experience from my own life to tell you that may be very illuminating because it concerns obsessive thoughts and worrying about money and income.

The last time I was in Hong Kong I was walking back to my hotel room after a long day working. I had eaten my evening meal, and was looking forward to a nice hot shower and some quiet time. I was not particularly attentive to my surroundings because my mind was filled with thoughts about money, or the possible lack thereof. Would I earn enough to pay my hotel bill? Would I have enough over to settle the accounts that would be waiting for me back in New Zealand? Could I earn enough to print my next book?
All this filled my head as I walked past a Buddhist monk standing ever so calmly holding his rice bowl. I nodded in acknowledgement to him and he gently smiled back, and I kept on going. Them WHAM! It was if I hit an invisible brick wall. I could not take one more step.
I knew that I needed to return and place a financial offering in the monks rice bowl. As I placed the money in his rice bowl, our eyes met and I saw a depth of faith and trust that I

had never ever witnessed before. It was as if he transmitted a measure of his deep faith that the universe would always provide for him, into the seat of my soul. His shy gentle smile and a subtle incline of his head in thanks was all that as necessary.

I then went upon my way. About 20 paces on I stopped to look back and view him for the last time, and he was nowhere to be seen. He had quite simply had vanished into thin air.

When I got to my hotel room and pondered over the experience, all I could see was the soft glowing face of the current Dalai Lama. His thoughts flooded my consciousness with the understanding that I should never fret over material things. His wisdom washed over me and through me reaching every corner of my mind. The experience seemed timeless and yet was probably no more than a couple of minutes in duration.

I was to be forever changed by this wonderful man, and his example of being a monk with a rice bowl, living in total faith that the universe would always provide for him.

This divine spiritual teacher has visited me many times over the years, and here he was, yet again, this time manifesting himself into physical form.

How else, at that precise time in my growth, when I needed it the most, could he teach me about a facet of the universal law of "Letting Go and Letting God".

The experience often returns to my consciousness to remind me that all material things are fleeting and of no consequence in the big scheme of things. Since that time I have found it very easy to let money and material things pass through my life, savouring them for the time I have wanted or needed them, releasing them when the timing is necessary in order to move on.

Letting go of loved ones is the next area I want to address. God gave us people to nurture, love, cherish, honour and respect, not to own. Slavery has been abolished for a great many years, and yet so many people want to own or enslave their loved ones. Truthfully, all you can ever really do is share with people.

Early in a relationship, possessiveness can be masked as charm or adoration. The person appears to be one who loves deeply, is protective, very helpful, always there and even, as someone who can take care of you. All of these traits are honourable, admirable and desirable. However, tipped to an extreme, become possessiveness, jealously, controlling and extremely mentally, emotionally and spiritually unhealthy.

At the risk of oversimplifying a behaviour pattern that is extremely complex, possessiveness is a common characteristic in a person who has self-esteem problems. These people are usually lacking in natural and comfortable levels of self-image and self-confidence.
Often, if the pattern is extreme, they will become bullies in order to boost their own importance. Really, they are scared you will find out how flawed and insecure they really are and leave them. It is a self-fulfilling prophecy because usually, given time, partners or loved ones do leave them.

Possessiveness or jealously is a very crippling and stifling behaviour to live with, because it does not foster or encourage independence, self reliance, personal freedom or true love. If you are possessive of your children do some self-searching to find out why. Is your behaviour reflecting something about some experiences from your childhood? Why don't you trust people to live their own life and make their own decisions? Why are you afraid to let them go?

As parents, part of your growth from having your children, is to learn to love them enough to let them go, and get on with your own life. You cannot live your hopes, dreams and wishes through your children, because they came to live their dreams not yours.

Our children came to do greater things with their lives than us. If we force them to live within the constraints of our values, views, actions, we will, if taken to the extreme, be going backwards as a species. If Martin Luther King, Ghandi, Maggie Thatcher, Louis Pasteur, Leonardo de Vinci, William Shakespeare, Mohamed Ali and Florence Nightingale, had all lived their parent's views to life, where would be. It simply doesn't bear imagining.

You need to encourage your children to do more, different and even better things than you currently do or did. Encourage them to be independent, responsible, self reliant, loving, caring people. The kind of person you would love to share the rest of your life with. When you give someone the gift of universal unconditional love, they will feel free to be expand, grow, move and be themselves, and yet, they will always want to return to you, the person who gave them such a gift.

When I am working with mothers, I always suggest that they make a plan for their own life before the following events take place.
1)   Their last child goes to school, or
2)   Their youngest child turns 14 to 16.
The reasoning behind this is that their lives will not bear such a burden of grief or loss when these events take place. If you start night classes, gym, or further education before all your children leave home, you are reclaiming your right to invest in yourself again.

It will make the transition from nurturer and carer to independence, easier and much more exciting. You will be liberating yourself along with your children. Perhaps to be your own person, for the first time since you got married or started a family.

People often ask me how I have the courage to travel alone to all manner of interesting places. They ask things like,

"Don't you get scared travelling alone?"
To which my humorous response is
"Travelling alone, travelling alone, I wish. I have never ever had the luxury of an aircraft, bus, or train to myself. They are always full of unmet fellow travellers and potential friends"
For this degree of courage I have to pay tribute to my mum. My childhood, from the age of 9 to 13, is full of memories of playing with my brother on rivers banks, in the bush, walking or cycling into town and being away from home for hours and hours.

*It was hunger that usually brought me home. Years later, I asked my mother if she ever worried we'd get hurt or into trouble? She said "No! I always **knew** you would be okay". Because she trusted her own intuition, my Mum gave us the fantastic gift of personal freedom.*

Yes she worried about us, and I believe as teenagers we contributed to her having a great many grey hairs. However, for the most part she encouraged us to be independent resourceful beings. How I bless her for that, for I believe I would never have done many of the things I have, without the foundation of inner trust she allowed to unfold within me.

I feel the hardest lesson about letting go is when we lose a loved one. Death seems so final. Of course if you have a spiritual view to life you will know there is no such thing as death. We as with everything else on this planet are energy, and science tell us that energy cannot be created or destroyed, it just is. It can change its form like water into ice, or water into steam, or plants die and become compost, or caterpillars become butterflies. So we too, when it is our time, will leave our physical bodies, change form and become energy.

Death is the door to a new adventure, pathway, direction or evolution. Death is inevitable, so when it arrives why should it shock or surprise us. Letting go of loved ones who have passed on is eventually the best thing to do. Often the need to

hold onto someone is our own selfishness or self-centredness. We simply do not want to let our loved one go.
We can cling to them like a life raft, talking to them everyday, needing their presence to keep our strength. We wish they could return to us or may even curse them because they left us here on our own. These reactions are perfectly okay, normal and understandable, because they are all a part of the healing process called grieving. When, and only when, we realise the effect of our actions, (on our departed loved one) will we see the wisdom of letting go and letting god take care of them.

I was watching the "Dr Phil" television show when I heard a couple talking about their grief over the loss of a twin son at his birth. The surviving twin, Tom was 18 when I heard this story. Every time Tom had a major growth step or achievement they would mourn that Grant wasn't there. This took place over Tom's first steps, first day at school, sports events, and scholastic achievements. Everything Tom did was weighed against their grief over Grant and what he might have been or done.
 When it was pointed out that that they had been negating every moment of their surviving son Tom's life, with their grief over Grant. How could he ever measure up or succeed being compared to a ghost? It was very, very moving experience as I witnessed the dawning or revelation of the affects of their grief and action. They had been negating every moment of their surviving son Tom's life, with their grief over Grant.
It was then suggested that they might consider that Grant was great soul and great spiritual teacher. Could they consider that his passing was endeavouring to show them a spiritual view, perspective or lesson about life.
As Dr Phil spoke to them it became clear to them that their dead son Grant had been trying to teach them to let go, move on and honour the son they had.
 The other side of the situation was that every time they dwelt on Grant, his death, and their loss they held him back. He was

162

not free to move on to higher and greater things. He was unable to continue his spiritual quest until they set him free. There is a period or time to mourn a time to cry and a time to grieve and then there is the time to" let go and let god" and return to rejoice in life.

So how does one strengthen your ability to "Let Go and Let God" determine more in your life.
Frankly, there is no simple or easy way. This process, along with all your other spiritual growth, is indeed a process. You will arrive at new levels of faith, at times in small steps or at others in giant leaps, as you journey through your life.

Many years ago when I was ordained as a minister of the Peace Community Church, I was required to make the following commitment statement.
We were each, in turn, asked to face each point of the compass as we made our declaration. It was suggested that we make this commitment statement once a day for 14 days. Here is the declaration statement we made. If, upon reading it, you are inspired to make the same commitment, please feel free to do so.

Spirit of the North I commit myself to myself and to my higher purpose
Spirit of the South I commit myself to myself and to my higher purpose
Spirit of the East I commit myself to myself and to my higher purpose
Spirit of the West I commit myself to myself and to my higher purpose
Spirit, Guide me, Use me, Let me be your instrument of love and wisdom.

All these years later, I feel it is still the greatest affirmation for letting the godhead guide someone who is serious about their own spiritual journey.

You see, it was designed with the aim to help a person rise above their limited perceptions about what they are doing here on earth. Thereby, assisting them to "Let go and let God, the universal masters and the divine oneness" guide their actions in all things.

A Teacher affects eternity
He can never tell where his influence stops

Your Changing Team

When you are newly awakened to the truth about your spiritual nature everything in your life, world and universe changes and will never be the same again. The truth is everyone is spiritual; it's just that some people are aware of it and some are not. This awakening stage is rather like you starting school. At this level of remembrance you will need a certain level of guide or teacher. One that is committed to helping you grasp and understand the spiritual basics.

As you invest time and energy in your personal spiritual growth and you begin to release the shackles of limiting thoughts and beliefs, you move to new levels of consciousness. This allows you access to new levels of guides and teachers.

The more opportunity you have for your actions and words to influence people, the higher the realms of universal knowledge that will be available to you. So much so, that it will seem as if your original team of Angels are no longer present. That familiarity that you had with your first guides and Angels will seem to fade or even disappear. You may even feel as if you have lost your connection. This, of course, will not be true. It simply means that you are now accessing levels of wisdom that are higher than your personal team.

It is a very long time since I have felt the very special and personal connection with my guides, Evette, Sister Serenity, Andrew and Franz. Even so! My heart knows they are always there for me and they rejoice at my connection with wisdom from higher sources. That being said, I can still recall the sound of their voices with great clarity. I can still feel the special vibration of love that each one flooded me with. They are as strong and clear in my heart memory today, as the day I first met them.

I cannot say with any form of proof, that I have changed teams and that my original team of helpers and I have completed the journey we began together. And yet I know this is true. I sense that we have completed the contract that we formed and now it is time for us all to evolve ever again.

As you continue your journey of growth, you will need to be able to talk to the masters and higher frequency beings than you required in the past. Whereas in the past I would speak to "my personal team" about how I could help another person. As I continue to expand and reach even greater numbers of people, whether it is through my column, counselling sessions, books or workshops, now comes from much higher realms and a vastly broader source.

The more you use "the bigger spiritual picture" in your life and therefore on those around you, then the more the universe will allow you to see, perceive and understand. If you are applying your innate sense of understanding and compassion to people's behaviours and situations, the more the masters will entrust you to "know" about the people you are assisting. It comes back to the core of all things, intention. If your intention is to help and empower people then you will be given insights that will expedite a positive outcome.

As we evolve so must those around us, and this includes our loved ones, friends, people at work and in our community. They must evolve and move with us, or leave our presence. I do not mean that they must act and think the same way as us, but rather allow us the freedom to be ever changing and evolving beings. As the evolution revolution takes place here on the earthly realms, the same thing is happening in the heavens.

To this end our original angelic team are divinely happy that we are now ready to receive wisdom and knowledge from the great ones. It is with joy that they celebrate "their job well done" as they bought us to this new point. They are suffused with light in the knowledge that together we have come that much closer to home called oneness.

So don't cling to your "specific" angels or guides, but rather give them the space to evolve from you. Grant them the freedom to move on if they wish, as you acquire and access other masters that were not available to you before. In my travels I hear some much possessive chatter or boasting about who,
> My first guide is.
> My special gatekeeper is.
> My healing angel is.
> The Master I channel is.

And I often look at such statements from the Angelic realms' point of view and wonder what would they think about such statements.
I wonder if I were an angelic being, how would I feel if the person I was "in charge of" said such things? Does my charge mean that if I do not have one of the above mentioned roles that;
> I am of no significance?
> That I cannot help?
> That my wisdom is considered of no value?
> That my spiritual contract to assist you is now invalid?

I am sure that this is not what the people mean or intend when they say such things, therefore it would be wise to allow the universe to choose the masters and Angels it feels would serve your highest good. Don't get stuck in a possessive attachment to anyone in heaven. Of course, this is a very good policy to activate on earth as well.

Give yourself the opportunity to connect with beings that hitherto have not been available to you. Welcome the chance to connect with new masters and light beings. Be open to meeting new beings and even be pro-active by asking if you can connect with a master that you would like to have a personal experience with. Allow yourself to experience the unlimited wonders that the universe has to offer.

Ask to be allowed the privilege to meet different master healers. Request an audience or conversation with a master of another culture. Ask to be shown the power of love. Seek an audience with the Lords of karma. Get in touch with the master beings that oversee a particular country. Above all have fun with all the great white spiritual beings that fill our universe.

All of God's Angels are watching over thee

You are a Light being

No matter how you see yourself, you are actually a being of energy and light. Your physical form will eventually fade into minute particles of dust and matter and you will be free to return home to the space place where you belong. This realm is often called heaven, the cosmos, the oneness, the all and the universe. No matter what we call it, it is still where we belong.

The universe sees you as a sacred spark of its own divinity and therefore as important as the sun, the moon and the stars. Its special perspective of you is always about how your love and understanding is adding to the oneness. You are a master light being who incarnated here on the earth realms to continue to expand your "lightness".

The more you "become yourself" the more radiant your light is. Therefore the more your physical form is imbued with the radiant white light. It is this light, wisdom and universal connection that allows you to help, heal, inspire, enthuse, assist, encourage and teach other people.

If you see yourself from a human perspective, you severely limit the degree of connection you can tap into. If you continue to see yourself as a parent, accountant, shop assistant, you limit "the more" that can be made from your journey here. The more you can accept yourself as a "light being" the stronger your connection with the universal realms will be.

If you find yourself in situations that are really testing your resolve to be positive and allow the universe to guide you, try using one of the following affirmations.

- I am a universal being of light, love and wisdom
- I am always guided by divine wisdom and light
- I am safe in God's hands
- I am a master light being no less than the moon and stars
- I am love and light
- I am always loved and accepted no matter what I choose to do
- The universe is always manifesting what is for my greatest good
- I am securely and safely held by Angels
- I am open to receive whatever is for my highest good

Then, whenever a worry or concern enters you head, like a cracked record, follow it with your chosen affirmation.
If it means that you have to say it in clusters of 3 several times a day, then that's what it means. It rather depends on how much hold your thoughts have on your head, time and energy. You will need to keep doing it until your mind runs freely again.

I was once given a very humorous piece of wisdom about negative thoughts and I love its relevance to this very day.
"There is no crime in thinking negative thoughts, it's entertaining them and inviting them to stay for lunch and dinner that is criminal".

You are here to practice living the universal spiritual laws. You already "know" all there is to know, you are simply re-discovering what you already know. Deep within yourself, you have all the answers you will ever need to live the life you choose.

You continue to be a divine light worker every time you do something that inspires or creates love, light, laughter, peace, forgiveness, encouragement, creativity, confidence and self belief in another individual.

Above all circumstances and experiences that make up the rich tapestry of your life, hold fast to the memory that you are a divine spark of loving light energy. You are now, always have been and always will be.

I am the Alpha and the Omega

You are Creating Heaven on Earth

We, meaning all human kind, are creating our world with our thoughts. So it follows that if we spend a great deal of our time connecting to the universal light realms we are creating our own version of "heaven on earth". Heaven is not a planet, star or place of any kind. It is a "thought" place, a perceived place.

If we have a belief that it is a place of lofty marbled halls, white robed people and constant divine music then that is what it is for us. The same follows for a version of hell. Neither heaven nor hell are places, but rather a state of mind. The divine intelligence that I call God once told me,
"Why should I bother to create a place like hell you people do a great job of creating one for yourselves".
A movie that demonstrates the concept of our beliefs creating our own versions of heaven and hell is the film that stars Robin Williams called "What dreams may come". I had to watch it three times to grasp the magnitude and significance of its message.

All things that are made into form began with a thought. Therefore our thoughts create our reality. What we believe comes into form. If we believe that our city is a dangerous place that is what we will see and experience. If we believe everyone is out to take advantage of us, then that is what will happen. Conversely, if we believe in the basic goodness of mankind, then, for the most part, we will be blessed by the goodness of people.

If we believe in the religious principle that we will be judged for our actions, now or when we pass on, then we will live a life full of fear and possible condemnation. We will create people to judge us and also find ourselves judging the lives of other people. The truth is God in its divine wisdom left the task of judging our actions to us and us alone. This intelligence said that, for the most part, we do a far more severe job of judging ourselves for our actions than it would ever dream of doing.

If we believe that God/Christ is all forgiving then we will be inclined to be forgiving of others and ourselves. If we believe we are one of the millions of divine light beings then so our lives will reflect that. We, as light beings are here to create Heaven on Earth.

We are here to add to, and anchor the light consciousness on the Earthly realms. Many light beings have incarnated in this time and space place with that very purpose in mind. Collectively, they have entered an incarnation on earth to bring about a major expansion in the mass level of consciousness. The aim is to bring it closer to the heavenly celestial consciousness.

These light beings have chosen many different avenues in which to bring about this major shift. You will see evidence of these great changes in understanding by the way we rally, as a world, to aid some disaster stricken country. Sir Bob Geldoff created a huge shift in consciousness when he launched his "Live Aid" concert all those years ago. Through the common bond of music he launched an unprecedented appeal to help our African brothers and sisters in need.

The help given to the South East Asian tsunami victims was yet another classic example of how we realise we are all brothers and sisters under the sun. Soon, there will come a time here on earth, when we can and will have the same understanding, concern and compassion for each other on a daily basis. Perhaps by then, we will not have the need for a disaster to unite and galvanise us into action.

Religious, economic, cultural, financial, educational and political barriers are coming down. We are moving towards a world where we can safely live and worship our god as we personally see fit. We are gaining in the ability to love and accept each other despite out differences.

Can you make a difference? YES, YES, YES. It must be said that you may not be called to be involved in world changing events, policies or activities. Be not disheartened, your contribution will be no less important. You can create your own heaven of earth by applying some simple spiritual guidelines for living. Not only can you change your own life, but also that of a town, a city and even a country. Inculcate the practice of,

- Loving and accepting your family, friends and neighbours.
- Judging no one, not even yourself.
- Be willing to forgive yourself and others for their actions.
- Encouraging people to live their own dreams and life plan.
- Sharing your spiritual wisdom to those who are willing to listen.
- Strive to be "more" of your divine self at all times.
- Pray, talk and listen to your God/Angels/Masters daily.

Do not belittle your, role in life, your paid task, nor your lack of education or opportunity. Heaven has hidden its master beings in the guise of mums and dads, sports coaches, refuse collectors, prisoners in jail, terminally ill children, homeless people, street gang members equally alongside high profile people of all nations.

Heaven does not discriminate nor determine a person's power to effect goodness and positive change by the job they are paid to do. Heaven always listens to the heartbeat and intentions of the soul. When it is in harmony with the universal rhythms and timing, all things are possible. Each day, do what you can to create your small slice of heaven on earth and you will, along with any millions of other beings, be creating a heavenly air on earth.

**In Heaven, Angels are
No-one in particular**

About Julia Vazey

Today Julia is known as a Spiritual Educator and Counsellor, Newspaper Columnist, Author and Inspirational Speaker.

However it was back in the 1970's that Julia Vazey began travelling the world teaching people spiritual concepts, principles and methods. All of which were designed to connect them to their Angels and their own spiritual plan or purpose. Her message about how to work with angels eventually earned her the loving nickname, **"the Angel Lady"**.

Even while experiencing spinal cancer, Julia's spiritual experiences with her Angels and light beings continued as strong as ever. During her chemotherapy treatment she was called, once again, to write yet another book. Julia feels this connection with her Angels and the master light beings, was a major factor in her journey to wellness and remission. Being reminded of her spiritual plan and path and the opportunities she could be involved in, kept her focused and moving forward.

She is respected and admired by the thousands of people who have attended her workshops and seminars in New Zealand, Malaysia, Singapore, Australia, England, France, Germany, Scotland, Canada and Hong Kong.

Her countless Radio, Television, Newspaper and Magazine interviews have made her a powerful influence in the lives of hundreds of thousands of people. She believes,

"When people are offered inspiration, encouragement, along with a bigger picture about what they can do, ordinary folks can, and will, do the most extraordinary things. All we have to do is give people a chance.
When we empower people they are then free to decide, grow, develop, expand and live a life of their choosing".

Always do your best, for then no man
can ask more of you.

Printed in the United Kingdom
by Lightning Source UK Ltd.
127000UK00001B/67-72/A